Number 106
Summer 2005

New Directions for Evaluation

Jean A. King
Editor-in-Chief

Theorists' Models in Action

Marvin C. Alkin
Christina A. Christie
Editors

THEORISTS' MODELS IN ACTION
Marvin C. Alkin, Christina A. Christie (eds.)
New Directions for Evaluation, no. 106
Jean A. King, Editor-in-Chief

Microfilm copies of issues and articles are available in 16mm and 35mm, as well as microfiche in 105mm, through University Microfilms Inc., 300 North Zeeb Road, Ann Arbor, Michigan 48106-1346.

New Directions for Evaluation is indexed in Contents Pages in Education, Higher Education Abstracts, and Sociological Abstracts.

NEW DIRECTIONS FOR EVALUATION (ISSN 1097-6736, electronic ISSN 1534-875X) is part of The Jossey-Bass Education Series and is published quarterly by Wiley Subscription Services, Inc., a Wiley Company, at Jossey-Bass, 989 Market Street, San Francisco, California 94103-1741.

SUBSCRIPTIONS cost $80.00 for U.S./Canada/Mexico; $104 international. For institutions, agencies, and libraries, $175 U.S.; $215 Canada; $249 international. Prices subject to change.

EDITORIAL CORRESPONDENCE should be addressed to the Editor-in-Chief, Jean A. King, University of Minnesota, 330 Wulling Hall, 86 Pleasant Street SE, Minneapolis, MN 55455.

www.josseybass.com

Editorial Policy and Procedures

New Directions for Evaluation, a quarterly sourcebook, is an official publication of the American Evaluation Association. The journal publishes empirical, methodological, and theoretical works on all aspects of evaluation. A reflective approach to evaluation is an essential strand to be woven through every volume. The editors encourage volumes that have one of three foci: (1) craft volumes that present approaches, methods, or techniques that can be applied in evaluation practice, such as the use of templates, case studies, or survey research; (2) professional issue volumes that present issues of import for the field of evaluation, such as utilization of evaluation or locus of evaluation capacity; (3) societal issue volumes that draw out the implications of intellectual, social, or cultural developments for the field of evaluation, such as the women's movement, communitarianism, or multiculturalism. A wide range of substantive domains is appropriate for *New Directions for Evaluation;* however, the domains must be of interest to a large audience within the field of evaluation. We encourage a diversity of perspectives and experiences within each volume, as well as creative bridges between evaluation and other sectors of our collective lives.

The editors do not consider or publish unsolicited single manuscripts. Each issue of the journal is devoted to a single topic, with contributions solicited, organized, reviewed, and edited by a guest editor. Issues may take any of several forms, such as a series of related chapters, a debate, or a long article followed by brief critical commentaries. In all cases, the proposals must follow a specific format, which can be obtained from the editor-in-chief. These proposals are sent to members of the editorial board and to relevant substantive experts for peer review. The process may result in acceptance, a recommendation to revise and resubmit, or rejection. However, the editors are committed to working constructively with potential guest editors to help them develop acceptable proposals.

Jean A. King, Editor-in-Chief
University of Minnesota
330 Wulling Hall
86 Pleasant Street SE
Minneapolis, MN 55455
e-mail: kingx004@umn.edu

CONTENTS

EDITORS' NOTES

Evaluation theorists seem to be quite good at propounding how they think the evaluation world ought to work. Indeed, most of the literature of our field consists of assertions by theorists about how they believe that evaluation *should* be done. Sometimes we find articles that frame a point of view about one particular aspect of evaluation. For instance, a theorist might proclaim the benefits of stakeholder participation in an evaluation. Sometimes these assertions relate to a desired outcome, such as increased use or greater attention to user needs.

The literature is also replete with examples of evaluations that have been conducted. These exemplars of practice reflect a myriad of viewpoints on the proper manner for conducting an evaluation. For example, some studies are virtually identical to what one would consider "research" studies. They seek to pursue methods that increase possibilities of "generalizability." Other evaluations pay great heed to the process of more strongly engaging stakeholders by incorporating their perspectives and values into the evaluation.

However, we do very little as evaluators in conducting systematic inquiry *about* our field. What are the conditions under which different kinds of evaluation are most effective? What evaluation tools, techniques, or procedures lead to the highest level of evaluation use, accuracy, satisfaction, and other criteria? There have been several cries for reflection about evaluation. In particular, Henry and Mark (2003) issued such a call in a recent issue of *New Directions for Evaluation*. They note, "There is a serious shortage of rigorous, systematic evidence that can guide evaluation or that evaluators can use for self-reflection or for improving their next evaluation" (p. 69). These authors suggest an agenda for the study of evaluation. This agenda is framed in terms of different particular emphases—in essence, types of ways of doing research on evaluation.

One way of doing evaluation research that Henry and Mark suggest is through analog studies. These are described as "controlled studies, generally experiments, designed to reflect real-life, practice settings while allowing for experimental control in testing some hypotheses about a potential influence on evaluation practice or outcomes" (2003, p. 74). This kind of work, using simulations, was found in the studies of evaluation use conducted by Larry Braskamp, Robert Brown, and Dianna Newman (1982) and several of their colleagues. Simulation research on evaluation was also conducted by Arthur Granville (1977) and Larry Fish (1995), two former students of one of us. By and large, all of these studies investigated a single aspect of evaluation (for example, the background of the evaluator) and varied only by one variable in a scenario presented to subjects. The intent of this research was to determine the extent to which subjects placed credence in the evaluation findings or were motivated to make program changes. This was extremely worthwhile research. However, tightly controlled experimental studies have a certain artificiality to them, in part because of the need to be restricted in focus and in the amount of material presented. Moreover, like most other experimental studies, they require a large number of subjects. Thus, although conducting research related to evaluation is critical to the advancement of the field, it is extremely difficult.

Important insights about both theory and practice can also be obtained through a process of comparative analysis. Here, evaluation theorists' and practitioners' views and approaches are subjected to thoughtful and systematic examination. The recent book *Evaluation Roots* (Alkin, 2004) provides a comparative vision of evaluation approaches by having selected authors lay out their views. The presentation of their points of view is a type of comparative analysis of evaluation theorists. In that instance, the comparative analysis is based on the things that theorists *say* they would do in conducting an evaluation. However, the authors were describing their theoretical views, unconstrained by the context and exigencies of field practice.

Yet do we really know that what theorists say they would do in practice is indeed what they would actually do? Evaluation, after all, is situational. Each context offers its own constituencies, set of values, programmatic elements, bureaucratic hurdles, and other elements. Evaluators need to adapt their point of view to a particular situation, and the way in which they make those adaptations is in fact an area that needs to be studied.

Deborah Fournier, in an excellent chapter on establishing evaluative conclusions (1995), points out that there are different working logics intrinsic to each evaluation approach. Within the working logic are to be found "phenomena of applicability"—situations in which their logic is likely to be appropriate. Thus, theorists describing their approach may have in mind different programs to be evaluated (or different ways of perceiving these programs).

So to do a good comparative analysis (or research study) on evaluation approaches, there must be some guidelines. It would perhaps be best if a number of evaluators each evaluated the same program. Obviously this is not feasible. There is often barely enough money available to do one good evaluation, let alone two or more on the same program and to do them simultaneously. Moreover, there is a great likelihood that simultaneous evaluations would confound each of the evaluation studies.

An example where specific situations are considered in determining evaluator strategy and approach is found in the Ethical Challenges section of the *American Journal of Evaluation*. In this series, Michael Morris, the section editor, poses a brief hypothetical case situation, and several evaluators indicate their approach to resolving that ethical dilemma (for example, see Morris, 2005; Mabry, 2005; Cousins, 2005). In these situations, the focus is only on ethical issues, and the case scenario is very brief.

A classic publication by the Association for Supervision and Curriculum Development, *Applied Strategies for Curriculum Evaluation* (Brandt,

1981), offers another example in which analogues were used for comparative analysis of evaluation practice. This publication presented a case study of the attempt by the "Radnor Middle School" to evaluate a humanities curriculum. The case study material included a report of the committee and a short history of the program's implementation. The purpose of this analogue was not research, but rather to teach about evaluation by showing how noted evaluation theorists would evaluate a particular program. In actuality, it is how they *say* they would evaluate the program. The participants included illustrious theorists such as Michael Scriven, Robert Stake, Elliot Eisner, and W. James Popham. Participants were asked to explain "in a general way" how they would evaluate this humanities curriculum.

This document, now long forgotten, provides inspiration for this *New Directions in Evaluation* volume. We present a somewhat more extensive case scenario than the Radnor case study as well as the views of four current evaluators in order to explicate the similarities and differences among them. What also is different is the attempt that subsequently will be made to systematically examine the extent to which there are practice differences among these theorists. Furthermore, we examine the extent to which practice differences were shaped by the theorists' perspectives (as explained in their published writings) and by the context presented in the case scenario.

In Chapter One, Nicole Eisenberg, Lynn Winters, and Marvin Alkin have authored a case description based on an actual program. In Chapter Two, Christina Christie and Tarek Azzam examine the writings of Jennifer Greene, Gary Henry, Stewart Donaldson, and Jean King to describe their theoretical perspectives. In the four subsequent chapters, Greene, Henry, Donaldson, and King describe an evaluation plan and the steps or procedures of the evaluation that each might propose. Chapter Seven affords an opportunity for these theorists to provide insights into the factors that shaped their evaluation response or were incompatible with their typical approach to evaluation. They address such topics as the extent to which the case context is similar (or not) to those that they typically evaluate and modifications of their typical approach required to fit this particular context.

The final chapter, by Marvin Alkin and Christina Christie, considers the theorists' proposed evaluations, as well as their subsequent comments, to develop themes related to the influence of theory and context on practice. Clearly, both the evaluator's theoretical dispositions and the nature of the evaluation situation have influence on how an evaluator would engage in practice. We allude not only to the particular design and methods suggested for use, but more broadly to how the evaluator chooses to construe the evaluation situation and the task at hand. We gain insights on this from the author comments in Chapter Seven. Also, we have asked the authors to comment on the synthesis in Chapter Eight.

Marvin C. Alkin
Christina A. Christie
Editors

References

Alkin, M. C. (ed.). *Evaluation Roots: Tracing Theorists' Views and Influences.* Thousand Oaks, Calif.: Sage, 2004.

Brandt, R. S. *Applied Strategies for Curriculum Evaluation.* Alexandria, Va.: Association for Supervision and Curriculum Development, 1981.

Braskamp, L. A., Brown, R. D., and Newman, D. L. "Studying Evaluation Utilization Through Simulations." *Evaluation Review,* 1982, 6(1), 114–126.

Christie, C. A. (ed.). *The Practice-Theory Relationship in Evaluation.* New Directions for Evaluation, no. 97. San Francisco: Jossey-Bass, 2003.

Cousins, J. B. "Commentary: Minimizing Evaluation Misuse as Principled Practice." *American Journal of Evaluation,* 2005, 25(3), 391–398.

Fish, L. "How Evaluators Perceive Evaluation Misuse." *Dissertation Abstracts International,* 1995, AAT9601283.

Fournier, D. M. "Establishing Evaluative Conclusions: A Distinction Between General and Working Logic." In D. M. Fournier (ed.), *Reasoning in Evaluation: Inferential Links and Leaps.* New Directions for Evaluation, no. 68. San Francisco: Jossey-Bass, 1995.

Granville, A. C. "Where Do School Decisions Really Come From?" *Dissertation Abstracts International,* 1977, AAT7716166.

Henry, G. T., and Mark, M. M. "Toward an Agenda for Research on Evaluation." In C. A. Christie (ed.), *The Practice-Theory Relationship in Evaluation.* New Directions for Evaluation, no. 97. San Francisco: Jossey-Bass, 2003.

Mabry, L. "Commentary: 'Gray Skies Are Gonna Clear Up.'" *American Journal of Evaluation,* 2005, 25(3), 385–390.

Morris, M. "Put on a Happy Face." *American Journal of Evaluation,* 2005, 25(3), 383–384.

MARVIN C. ALKIN *is an emeritus professor in the Social Research Methodology Division in the Graduate School of Education and Information Studies at the University of California, Los Angeles.*

CHRISTINA A. CHRISTIE *is an assistant professor and associate director of the Institute of Organizational and Program Evaluation Research at Claremont Graduate University.*

1

The Bunche–Da Vinci case presents a situation at Bunche Elementary School that the four theorists were asked to address in their evaluation designs.

The Case: Bunche–Da Vinci Learning Partnership Academy

Nicole Eisenberg, Lynn Winters, Marvin C. Alkin

Bunche–Da Vinci Learning Partnership Academy is an elementary school located between an urban port city and a historically blue-collar suburb. The dignified and well-maintained school structure is a much-sought-after refuge for students, both African American and Latino, from the neighboring smaller suburb, well known for poverty, crime, racial tension, and low-performing schools. The school is a beacon of hope and stability in an industrial area of the large city and contrasts sharply with the nearby schools of the smaller, more notorious, adjacent suburb. Bunche is a "lighthouse" created by a unique partnership between the district and a nonprofit educational company specializing in innovative school interventions for low-performing students. The district recognized early on that to combat the problems that Bunche's students face, innovative solutions were needed. The school is characterized by students with a high transiency rate, illegal enrollments from the adjacent district, and high numbers of non-English-speaking students, a young and inexperienced staff with high turnover, and geographical isolation from the rest of the district. When approached by Da Vinci Learning Corporation, the district chose Bunche Academy to enter into a unique arrangement with the company to create a partnership that combined elements of a charter school while still remaining a regular part of the district.

The Community

Bunche–Da Vinci is located in an industrial zone on the northwestern edge of a city of half a million. Students travel several miles and must cross busy boulevards to reach the site; thus, most arrive on district school buses. The

NEW DIRECTIONS FOR EVALUATION, no. 106, Summer 2005 © Wiley Periodicals, Inc.

homes in the community are mostly small ranch houses from the 1940s and boxy modern 1950s apartment buildings. Many of the dwellings house multiple families or families with several children. There are no supermarkets, department stores, or large shopping malls in the community. Most shopping is done in small, expensive mom-and-pop grocery stores, located in corner strip malls housing the predictable fast food chains, liquor stores, and check cashing services found in poor neighborhoods.

The School

Bunche–Da Vinci Learning Partnership Academy remains part of the large urban school district but is also a partnership with the Da Vinci Learning Corporation. Da Vinci is a "full-service school reform operation" that has been partnering with Bunche for the past three years. Schools owned or operated by Da Vinci must adhere to its curriculum, schedules, and class size requirements. Bunche is the only school working with Da Vinci that retains its autonomy from the corporation and is wholly run by a school district. Teachers work 205 days (as opposed to the regular teacher year of 185), and the school year is 200 days (as opposed to 180). Students attend an extended day, six to eight hours in length. Classrooms for kindergarten through grade 3 are staffed at a ratio of 20:1; grades 4 and 5 are staffed at 35:1, with a 20:1 ratio during the extended reading period.

Students are grouped and placed by ability, regardless of grade level. This means that during reading and math, students are grouped by the grade level at which they are functioning. (For example, a fifth grader reading at the first-grade level goes to the grade 1 reading group). Every student receives a full curriculum: reading, math, language arts, science, social studies, music, art, physical education, modern foreign languages, and values education. The elective program is handled in two ways. Reading teachers, who are specialists, also teach music, art, physical education, or modern languages. Homeroom teachers teach math, language arts, social studies, science, and values education. Students receive specialized instruction one to two periods a day. K–2 teachers do planning outside their school day. Teachers in grades 3 to 5 have a planning period built into the school day, which runs from 8:30 to 4:30.

Da Vinci Learning focuses heavily on providing technology-rich environments for students and teachers. All teachers receive personal laptops and PDAs (personal digital assistants) while working at the school. All grade reporting and classroom bookkeeping are done online and hosted at Da Vinci. Students have multiple opportunities to work with computers and take computer-assisted tests beginning in grade 2. The school's mission statement is: "Excellence for All; Excuses for None."

The combination of state and federal funding provides Bunche with an annual operating budget in excess of $8 million. The school, with 1,150 students, receives a $5,200 per pupil allocation yearly from the state. These state revenues are used mainly to cover salaries. The remaining operating funds come from indirect services provided by the district or from categorical funds. Specifically, Title I funding adds an additional $2 million. Education Foundation gifts, Title III, and grant funds make up about 10 percent of the school's budget. Da Vinci has full control of the funds as part of its partnership agreement and uses them to staff lower class sizes, fund the extended school day and year, provide technology, and pay teachers.

Enrollment at Bunche has been steadily rising over the past few years due to an influx of Latino families into this historically African American neighborhood. Many of the new Latino families are fleeing the adjacent suburb in search of safer neighborhoods and better schools. Prior to the Partnership, Bunche enrolled about 1,050 students. With the advent of the partnership, enrollment dipped to 900, but in the second year, which coincided with an influx of Latino immigrants, it surged to 1,150 and is steadily growing by about 100 students a year. Bunche has always served low-income families, but the demographics have shifted dramatically over the past ten years (see Table 1.1).

Bunche has a large portion of students who are not fluent English speakers. Almost 60 percent of the school population is classified as English language learners (ELLs), with 97 percent of those being Spanish speakers. A little more than half of these ELL students are mainstreamed—that is, they are part of the regular classes—with extra support provided. The remaining students are enrolled in Structured English Immersion for a portion of the day and then mainstreamed with support for the rest of the day. Aside from the Structured English Immersion program, there are no other "pull-outs." That is, Title I and other funded programs are schoolwide programs, where students remain in class and are not pulled out for special instruction.

Student test scores at Bunche have been among the lowest in the district for many years. Teachers note that issues of how to teach ELLs dominate faculty lounge chat and faculty meetings. Secondary concerns about the neighborhood and classroom tension between African American and Latino students, even at this young age, also consume time and attention and remain the focus of the values education program. However, students apparently are delighted to come to and remain in school, a place where they feel safe, have access to computers, and participate in organized after-school arts activities.

Table 1.1. Bunche Enrollment Trends, 1995–2004: Percentage Distribution by Ethnicity

	Hispanic	African American	Asian, Filipino, Pacific Islander	White	American Indian
1995	54.2	25.2	16.3	3.5	0.8
2004	78.7	17.2	3.3	0.7	0.1

A New Principal

Bunche was converted from a somewhat bland elementary school in a remote corner of the district to an innovative experiment in public-corporate partnership. With the advent of the partnership, the district assigned a new principal to Bunche–Da Vinci, Mary García, in hopes of signaling to the community that this was a fresh start. García was a first-year principal but hardly an inexperienced administrator. In keeping with past practice, the district assigned staff to the principalship only after they had experience at both inner-city and suburban school sites, as well as the central office. García had spent seven years teaching at a nearby K–8 school in both the upper elementary and middle school grades. She had spent three years in district office assignments in both the Special Projects (Title I, Title III) and Curriculum offices, where she worked as a literacy coach. García is cheerful by nature, but beneath her ready smiles and warm manner lies fierce determination to level the playing field for her poorest and most struggling students. She has strong opinions regarding issues of equity and quality instruction and can be quite tough. In addition, she has always been known to focus on what is best for children over what is best for teachers when these values are in conflict.

Because she had spent many years working in the neighboring schools and the central office, she was well aware of the conditions and challenges facing her in her first year as principal. As is often the case in elementary schools, the staff of seventy-two teachers and specialists was predominantly young, and the majority had young children at home. Each year brought at least two engagements, two marriages, and three pregnancies. In terms of ethnicity, almost half the teachers and support staff were Hispanic, slightly fewer were white, and six were African American. Over half of the teachers were bilingual. Though not staffed with all beginning teachers, teaching staff was nonetheless young. Teachers had an average age of thirty and approximately four years of experience.

García found that parents and students were enthusiastic about the school and supportive of the programs. Teachers, in contrast, complained of feeling "burned out" and "jerked around" by the long school day, extended year, and "imported" curriculum. The teachers' union had met with the principal at least once a year at the request of fourth-grade teachers who felt the schedule was "grueling" and the Da Vinci curriculum "constricting." Both sides were watching test scores as a way to vindicate their positions.

Staff felt they had no extra time to attend PTA meetings at night (and the neighborhood was not an inviting place to be after dark). The PTA, in fact, barely existed. A handful of parents, often accompanied by small children, met monthly to plan refreshments for the annual Teachers Day and Back-to-School Night and to schedule the monthly Parent Education meetings with the district parent education coordinator. Although the majority of parents spoke Spanish, meetings were conducted in English, and no translator was provided.

García's first action at Bunche was to make it clear in faculty meetings that a new spirit was going to be injected into the school and the new direction would be a product of what she called "joint decision making." Her belief was that to a large extent, the students' success in school would depend on the confidence and support of the teachers—the "self-fulfilling prophesy" approach. She wanted to make this prophesy positive: "We have the special skills to teach these children, and only we can turn them around." García stressed the attitude that "all roads lead to Rome" and that even with an "external" curriculum and a multitude of subjects that didn't "count" for No Child Left Behind (NCLB) accountability, Bunche–Da Vinci students could succeed.

During the partnership's first year, the new principal and her staff spent numerous sessions reviewing school data on state and district assessments and discussing possible strategies. They agreed that the school's top priority should be reading: that was clearly where students were having difficulty. Historically, this school's reading test scores had been below the state average, and the proportion of students in the bottom ranges was higher than in most other schools in the district.

Early data suggested that some of their efforts paid off. During the first two years of the partnership, student scores on state tests showed improvement, and they were able to meet their Adequate Yearly Progress targets, as set by NCLB. However, García worried because she felt this was merely surface improvement. It was true that there was some progress from year 1 to year 2. However, after the second year of the partnership, only 29 percent of the students scored at a level considered "Proficient" in English–Language Arts, which was below the district and state average. In addition, García worried about the performance of specific subgroups of students. For example, when examining ethnic groups, she noted that only 28 percent of the Hispanics and 25 percent of the African American students were Proficient. Equally disturbing was the fact that fully one-third of the students were scoring in the bottom range of the state tests.

Challenges and Unfinished Business

Despite the initial small gains in state test scores, García felt that many problems remained at the school. The hope was that the school was on the right track. But then she received new results from the latest state test scores and found that despite the initial improvement, the partnership's third-year scores had gone down. (Table 1.2 shows the percentage of students for each subgroup scoring at the Proficient level in the English–Language Arts state standards tests for the three years of the partnership.) The data indicate that English language scores dropped to a level below first-year scores, completely nullifying the small spark of optimism that García had felt. All groups had shown a drop in scores, with perhaps the greatest decline for African American students.

Table 1.2. Bunche–Da Vinci Partnership Test History: Percentage Proficient on State Standards Tests for English-Language Arts

	Year 1	Year 2	Year 3
All	28	29	24
Hispanic	27	28	25
African American	23	25	20
White	75	72	65
Asian	80	85	78
ELL	22	21	20
Low socioeconomic status	30	29	27
Special education	10	8	7

Moreover, these decreasing state test scores contrasted sharply with students' performance on Da Vinci's own testing system. Da Vinci Learning Corporation tested students on a regular basis, and on Da Vinci's standardized tests, students had improved considerably. The percentage of students reading at grade level had doubled over the past three years. Da Vinci staff from headquarters, who were sent to monitor the curriculum, indicated that they had heard students say that they were "finally able to read" and found that even quite mature fifth-grade students who were working in grade one materials were enthusiastic learners. García wondered why this mismatch occurred.

Her first thought was that perhaps it was an issue of misalignment. She knew that the school's staff often had difficulty aligning the Da Vinci reading curriculum with the state standards. The Da Vinci program emphasized sustained silent reading, literature, invented spelling, and group work. This approach diverged considerably from the state-adopted program that emphasized whole-class direct instruction, phonics, spelling lessons, and continuous assessment and reteaching.

But was it just the alignment, or was it more than that? García knew that parents and students were, overall, happy with the school. But she did not feel the same level of support from teachers. Like many other schools in low-income neighborhoods, the staff turnover was high. But these teachers were especially resentful of teachers in other district schools, even their year-round neighbors. They rarely stayed once they had opportunities to teach in a traditional calendar school. The long hours, required in-service, shorter vacation time, and additional teaching assignments were wearing teachers down despite the additional pay. Fully 25 percent of the teachers had emergency credentials, and another 30 percent were teaching outside their subject areas due to the requirements that the school offer foreign language, values education, and technology classes. With the inception of NCLB, these teachers were required to be fully certified in their subjects by taking courses or tests. The result was that fully 60 percent of the faculty had outside commitments after school and on weekends in order to meet these requirements. Among the faculty, 65 percent had been teaching fewer than three years. They were enthusiastic, idealistic, and committed to the proposition that all students can learn, but few had enough experience to implement a rigorous or even accelerated curriculum for students who were underprepared or were English learners. They were literally learning how to "fly the plane while building it," which created a climate of alternating high hopes and frustration depending on the day. García had a tightrope to walk between offering encouragement and raising the bar. There were very real demands on the teachers in terms of learning a new curriculum, trying to make the curriculum align to the state testing system, learning to teach, taking required courses, attending to their own small children, and knowing that they were the only school in the district with such a workload (despite being compensated for it).

García was also concerned about teachers' time on task. For one thing, she felt too much of the extended day was devoted to computer-assisted instruction. A chief goal of this instruction was to individualize instruction better, but teachers had difficulty using the cumbersome and overwhelming "diagnostic" data, which rarely mapped onto strategies and skills used by the reading program or the state standards. In the face of conflicting information about students, teachers used their own judgment and impressions to regroup students in reading and math. But the computer-based activities were only part of it. García had a hunch that teachers were not spending enough time on reteaching and accelerating the learning of the lowest-performing students.

Something else was worrying García. She noted that during the partnership's second year, there were more changes in the student population than she had anticipated. This third year, she was again amazed by the number of new students and by the large bulk of students who left. Was this having any effects or negative influences on the classroom?

García knew that for the most part, parents were satisfied with the school. However, there were a few parents who questioned the amount of time that children spent "on the computer." Recently she had received a surprise visit from a group of six Title I parents. They had arrived in her office one morning to complain about the situation. Their children were among the lowest-achieving students and were having difficulty learning to read. These parents agreed that the technology was good, but felt that it should not be "taking time away" from the "more necessary reading lessons."

García empathized with those parents. The plight of the below-grade-level student had become the principal's top concern. But she was not sure whether the parents' attributions were correct. Faculty struggled to serve these students but often could not see ways in which they could change their instruction. Not all students had made the reading gains that most of the Filipino, white, and native-born Hispanic students had, even though attendance was relatively high for all subgroups of students. Few teachers discerned this until García pointed it out to them. Even then, faculty tended to dismiss out of hand their responsibility for the differences in reading performance. When reviewing annual test results for subgroups of students, teachers could often be heard saying, "Oh, he's never here. His family takes him to Mexico for weeks at a time." Or, "She was new to the district. Entered way behind. Of course, she scores low." And the ubiquitous, "You should see their family situation. It's a miracle that child comes regularly."

The principal felt that the school had just scratched the surface in addressing the literacy problem. Test results showed that students still struggled with spelling and editing skills, composition, and reading comprehension of nonfiction text, not to mention that mathematics had been all but ignored during the year's work on schoolwide literacy. While the Da Vinci Learning curriculum was moderately effective in developing conceptual understanding, students did poorly on the state tests due to lack of fluency with number facts and procedures.

García felt that she and her staff could not tackle the school's difficulties alone. There were aspects about the partnership that she questioned, but she lacked the skills to assess whether she was right. She felt that the school and the partnership needed to undergo some changes. She needed to think about a course of action and then meet to discuss them with the district superintendent.

After careful thought, she contacted the district superintendent, Douglas Chase. Chase was a home-grown superintendent. He was born in the community and had attended elementary, intermediate, and high school in the community. He had received a Ph.D. in policy from a nationally acclaimed research university, moved across the country to teach in higher education in a major urban center, and had an extensive national collegial network encompassing foundations and government officials. He was a visionary with keen political instincts and a lateral thinker who prized diversity in thought and style. He was a passionate advocate for poor children and not content to wait generations for results. One of his favorite aphorisms was, "It's five minutes to midnight." Chase's most prominent characteristic was his novel view on age-old problems. His staff knew that whenever they asked a question, they would not be able to predict the response: it would represent a vision, a stance, a viewpoint, or a question they had not thought about before.

Chase had been at the district for many years and had witnessed Bunche–Da Vinci's changes over time. He had initially advocated in favor of the partnership, realizing that the district alone could not do much more to help schools such as Bunche. However, over time, he too had developed questions about the partnership. He had overheard some of his staff talk about the problems at Bunche–Da Vinci and was wondering whether it might be best to end the contract. With his down-to-business style, he focused on test results, which had declined in the past year. That was what he really cared about. He wondered whether the initial increase in test scores (during the partnership's first two years) was a result of the actual partnership and Da Vinci's "research-based curriculum," or of the district-provided in-service and staff development.

García and Chase met a few times to discuss what they could do. Initially Chase wondered if the innovative partnership was part of the problem. García knew it was too early to know and asked to work with Da Vinci in a more collaborative (and less "obedient") fashion. Chase also wondered if the district needed to provide more and different support to the novel enterprise. He knew that staff—by their very attitudes—could go through the motions yet undermine the most promising of innovations. García, a can-do and well-regarded professional, felt that installing systems in place—for teacher collaboration, monitoring curriculum and instruction, student interventions, and even communication with Da Vinci—would go a long way toward righting the ship. Chase, never a micromanager, was more than willing to allow her to work the partnership her way for the coming year (or two at most).

Chase was open to giving García time to resolve Bunche's problems, but also wanted more data. He wanted to know why there was a disparity in Da Vinci and state test scores. He wanted to know if the Da Vinci curriculum was manageable. He had other questions as well, but he also recognized that he wanted to give García the flexibility to make changes. He wanted to support her in her efforts, and to do so she would need evaluation help, not only to monitor the impact of her changes but also as a reliable source of evaluative data on the impact of the program or parts of it.

Chase knew that the district evaluation unit was very small and was overworked on Title and other special programs. Thus, he decided that an outside evaluation might be appropriate. He suggested that García call DGHK Evaluation Associates to ask for an evaluation and recommendations for school improvement. Chase indicated that he would find funds from one of his foundation sources for an external evaluation. García was all too eager to comply with the request for an evaluation; she hoped that it would help her in making improvements to the program.

NICOLE EISENBERG is a doctoral student in the Social Research Methodology Division in the Graduate School of Education and Information Studies at the University of California, Los Angeles.

LYNN WINTERS is the assistant superintendent of research, planning, and evaluation in the Long Beach Unified School District in California.

MARVIN C. ALKIN is an emeritus professor in the Social Research Methodology Division in the Graduate School of Education and Information Studies at the University of California, Los Angeles.

2

The authors describe and compare the four theoretical perspectives represented by the theorists writing Chapters Three through Six, providing additional comparative analysis based on their published works.

What Theorists Say They Do: A Brief Description of Theorists' Approaches

Christina A. Christie, Tarek Azzam

Perhaps now more than ever before, funders are requesting that social and educational programs be evaluated for accountability and to demonstrate effectiveness. This is great news for the discipline and for those conducting evaluations because this mandate translates into, by and large, greater value for our work and an increased opportunity for evaluators to practice our craft. With increased occasion to evaluate, we are more likely to encounter greater diversity in the types of programs we are studying. How, then, does one determine the best evaluation design? The evaluation theory literature provides a myriad of approaches to help inform this decision and subsequently guide evaluation design and implementation. The question remains about how a theory will translate into practice.

The purpose of this volume is to examine, comparatively, the practical application of theorists' approaches to evaluation by examining four evaluations of the same case. The thought is that when asked to evaluate the same program (holding the case constant), the practical distinctions between theorists' approaches become evident. We would also speculate that subtler differences in approaches will be highlighted, and surprising similarities will emerge. For this exercise to prove profitable, theorists must be proponents of approaches that are, from the outset, different and that these differences will remain evident in their practice.

Who Was Invited and Why: Theorist Selection

We are fortunate that the four distinguished scholars invited to participate in our exercise—Jennifer Greene, Gary Henry, Stewart Donaldson, and Jean King—all agreed to take part. When selecting theorists for participation, the editors were committed to inviting only theorists who are actively evaluating programs. Most of those who offer theoretical views on evaluation have conducted evaluations. We were concerned, however, that theorists with more limited or less current experience would be inclined to reiterate their theoretical writings rather than explain what they would actually *do* when confronted with designing an evaluation for our case school, Bunche–Da Vinci.

It can be difficult to translate into text some of the more nuanced aspects of a theoretical approach. Thus, another criterion used when selecting the evaluation scholars for this volume was contemporary and, more important, accessible theoretical writings. It was our hope that theorists whose writings are more easily understood by broad audiences would be more likely to translate their theoretical approaches into readable evaluation designs.

Using Taxonomies

Evaluation theory classification schemas systematically and thoughtfully group together and distinguish approaches based on an articulated set of criteria. The editors wanted to ensure, as much as possible, that differences in approaches would emerge when described in our exercise. With these criteria in mind, we turned to theoretical classification schema to guide our selection of theorists for this volume.

Evaluation theoretic approaches are often better understood when classified by defining features or characteristics. There are several well-known classification schemas, such as those put forth by Fitzpatrick, Sanders, and Worthen (2003), Shadish, Cook and Leviton (1991), and Alkin and House (1992). Alkin and Christie (2004) recently published their own classification schema, the evaluation theory tree. This taxonomy uses three principal dimensions of evaluation—methods, values, and use—to categorize approaches based on their primary emphasis.

Although only one of our four theorists (King) is represented in Alkin and Christie's published schema, we found that examining each perspective within the context of this particular taxonomy illustrates the diversity of theoretical perspectives represented by our theorists. It also provides an opportunity to consider what distinguishes each of these theorists. Our analysis places Donaldson on the methods branch, Greene on the values branch, and King on the use branch. Henry, through his writings (Mark, Henry, and Julnes, 2000), showed that he would not easily be placed in the methods, value, or use category.

Greene is a proponent of a value-engaged approach to evaluation and has been in the forefront of advancing both the discussion and application of this approach. This approach incorporates elements of responsive evaluation with principles from democratic evaluation. Value-engaged evaluation is responsive to the particulars of the evaluation context (Stake, 1980) while including relevant interests, values, and views so that conclusions can be unbiased in value as well as factual aspects (House and Howe, 2000). The approach relies heavily on the values of those involved in the program, including program recipients.

The methods branch of the tree represents theoretical approaches that are grounded in, and have a primary emphasis on, social science methodology. Donald Campbell anchors this branch, from which all method branch theories have been derived. Henry, who generally evaluates large-scale education programs with an eye toward policy reform, espouses emergent realist evaluation (ERE) theory (Mark, Henry, and Julnes, 1998, 2000). This contingency-based approach aimed at social betterment generally lends itself to quantitative methods of inquiry, such as fully randomized experiments and quasi-experiments. Therefore, when investigating causation, Henry advocates using a randomized controlled trial whenever feasible. When experiments are not viable, Henry is most likely to turn to the less rigorous but often more practical quasi-experimental designs to study program effectiveness. In addition to Henry's writings on ERE, he has authored several noted contributions on sampling and other techniques necessary for and concerned with conducting good experiments. In addition, in the reports from studies Henry has conducted, his emphasis and his belief in the value for experimental methods is evident.

Donaldson is best known for his work in the area of theory–driven evaluation (TDE). Thus, Donaldson would be placed further up the methods branch, positioned next to Huey Chen. (In the context of the theory tree, moving up a branch reflects the evolution of theoretical approaches, away from, but still grounded in, the initial theoretical approaches and thinking that served as the foundation for, and are positioned at the base of, the branch.) Early TDE thinking was put forth by two of evaluation's most illustrious theorists, Carol Weiss and Peter Rossi (see Weiss, 1998; Rossi and Freeman, 1993), both of whom are on the methods branch of the theory tree. Their initial ideas were expounded on by Huey Chen, who published the first text dedicated exclusively to this approach (Chen, 1990) and is frequently recognized for ushering TDE into its prominent place in the evaluation theory literature. Donaldson refers to his variety of TDE as *program theory–driven evaluation science*.

King is concerned most with use of the evaluation process and its results. Her emphasis is not only on use, but also participation in the evaluation process as a means for increasing use and building internal program evaluation capacity. Her approach evolves most directly from participatory evaluation and extends the notions of Cousins and Whitmore (1998) by particularly emphasizing the importance of building evaluation capacity. Although Cousins is also concerned with building evaluation capacity through participation in the evaluation process, it is his secondary rather than his principal interest. King is concerned primarily with building evaluation capacity as a principal outcome for the evaluation. She argues that increasing evaluation capacity is essential for promoting and ensuring evaluation use. Stakeholder participation is requisite for achieving this goal. King has written extensively about her experiences implementing her approach, interactive evaluation practice, not only as an external but also as an internal evaluator for a midwestern school district.

Brief Descriptions of the Theorists' Approaches

Jennifer C. Greene. Greene is an advocate of a value-engaged approach to evaluation, which incorporates responsive (Stake, 1980, 1987) and democratic (House and Howe, 2000) processes to study social and educational programs. Her approach is responsive in that the evaluation design is developed in response to the program context. It is democratic in that it places great importance on considering the perspectives and values of all legitimate stakeholders, especially stakeholders who are typically alienated from evaluation processes (House and Howe, 2000). Greene (2000) argues that evaluations can be "used to surface and legitimate differing views and values and move [stakeholder] towards shared understanding of the values of educational outcomes" (p. 16).

Greene offers three "justifications" for including stakeholder views when conducting evaluations: (1) pragmatic justification, (2) emancipatory justification, and (3) deliberative justification. The *pragmatic* justification argues for stakeholder inclusion because it increases the chance of evaluation use (Patton, 1997) and organizational learning (Preskill and Torres, 1999). The *emancipatory* justification focuses on the importance of acknowledging the skills and contributions of stakeholders and empowering them to be their own social change agents (Fettermen, 2001). The *deliberative* justification argues that evaluation should serve to ensure that program or policy conversations include all relevant interests and are "based on the democratic principles of fairness and equity and on democratic discourse that is dialogic and deliberative" (Greene, 2000, p. 14).

Greene's methodical approach to the evaluation process reflects her interest in representing the values of differing stakeholders. She prefers to incorporate a mix of qualitative and quantitative methods (Greene and Caracelli, 1997), which can answer both broad and in-depth evaluation questions. Based on experiences during a previous program evaluation, Greene argues that the use of mixed methods should be defensible politically, philosophically, and technically (Greene and Caracelli, 1997). (In this evaluation, which is discussed in depth in Greene, 2000, stakeholders argued and clashed over the validity of the methods used and were not able to focus on discussions of values or reach any kind of meaningful consensus.) Her approach when conducting an evaluation is guided by principles of inclusion, dialogue, and deliberation. Implementation of these principles is intended to "extend impartiality by including relevant interests, values, and views so that conclusions can be unbiased in value as well as factual aspects"

(House and Howe, 2000, p. x). In the context of the guiding principles, the evaluator is responsible for systematic and unbiased data collection, analysis, and presentation of findings.

Gary T. Henry. The ultimate goal of evaluation, social betterment, drives the ERE approach proposed by Mark, Henry, and Julnes (1998, 2000). ERE focuses on understanding the underlying mechanisms of programs and thus is concerned primarily with addressing the research questions that help identify program mechanisms that are operating and those that are not (Mark, Henry, and Julnes, 1998). The ERE evaluator develops a study in an attempt to understand causality rather than being satisfied with a description of program outcomes. As a result, the ERE evaluation attempts not only to identify well-functioning program mechanisms, but also to enhance the generalizable knowledge base of a particular set of programs or program theories.

The emergent realist evaluator takes into account program effects that are of most interest to the public and other relevant stakeholders and thus must determine stakeholders' values when investigating possible mechanisms. (This part reflects the attention given to the values of stakeholders when conducting and framing evaluation questions.) Henry (1996) argues that understanding the values of the various stakeholder groups, including areas of consensus and conflict, helps to promote democratic policy. ERE offers three methods for investigating stakeholder values. The first involves surveying and sampling possible stakeholders, and the second uses qualitative methods such as interviews or focus groups (or both) to determine their needs and concerns. The third approach involves analyzing the context of the evaluation from a broad philosophical perspective, focusing on issues such as equity, equality, and freedom. (This third approach is referred to as "critical analysis.") These value investigations should then be communicated to the multiple audiences of the evaluation (Mark, Henry, and Julnes, 1998).

The ERE evaluator also engages in a process of *competitive elaboration* or *principled discovery*. Competitive elaboration involves ruling out alternative explanations for study findings, which includes exploring alternative program theories and threats to validity (Mark, Henry, and Julnes, 1998). This requires a preexisting body of knowledge of possible program mechanisms and, ideally, a study design that experimentally tests each relevant mechanism to identify those with the greatest or least impact. (Relevant mechanisms are determined by a combination of stakeholder involvement and existing theories about a program.) This approach lends itself to quantitative methods of inquiry (such as fully randomized experiments and quasi-experiments). Principled discovery is used when programs are evaluated before practitioners are able to develop experientially tested theories (Mark, Henry, and Julnes, 1998). Approaches to discovering program mechanisms include exploratory data analysis (Tukey, 1977), graphical methods (Henry, 1995), regression analysis, and a context-confirmatory approach (Julnes, 1995). (Under the context-confirmatory approach, "an empirical discovery that suggests a mechanism is used to generate a distinct prediction that should be true if the newly induced mechanism is operating"; Henry, Mark, and Julnes, 1998, p. 14.)

Stewart I. Donaldson. Donaldson is a proponent of what he refers to as *program theory–driven evaluation science* (PT-DES). The phrase *program theory–driven* (instead of *theory driven*) is intended to clarify the meaning of the use of the word *theory* in the evaluation context of evaluation by attempting to specify the type of theory (for example, program theory, not necessarily social science theory) that is guiding the evaluation questions and design. Donaldson distinguishes between program theory and other types of theory, such as social science theory, and defines program theory as a theory of how program components are presumed to affect outcomes and the conditions under which these processes are believed to operate (Donaldson, 2001). *Evaluation science* (instead of evaluation) is intended to underscore the use of rigorous scientific methods (qualitative, quantitative, and mixed method designs) to attempt to answer valued evaluation questions. It also is intended to highlight the emphasis placed on the guiding principle of systematic inquiry (American Evaluation Association, 1995) and the critical evaluation standard of accuracy (Joint Committee on Standards for Educational Evaluation, 1994).

PT-DES is the systematic use of substantive knowledge about the phenomena under investigation and scientific methods to determine the merit, worth, and significance of evaluands such as social, educational, health, community, and organizational programs (Donaldson, forthcoming). Its application involves using program theory to define and prioritize evaluation questions and using scientific methods to answer those questions.

Donaldson offers a simple three-step model for understanding the basic activities of program theory–driven evaluation science:

1. Developing program theory
2. Formulating and prioritizing evaluation questions
3. Answering evaluation questions

Simply stated, evaluators typically work collaboratively with stakeholders to develop a common understanding of how a program is presumed to solve a problem of interest. Social science theory and prior research (if they exist) can be used to inform this discussion and assess the feasibility of the proposed relationships between a program and its desired initial, intermediate, and long-term outcomes (Donaldson and Lipsey, forthcoming). This common understanding of program theory helps evaluators and stakeholders identify and prioritize evaluation questions. Evaluation questions of most interest are then answered using the most rigorous scientific methods possible given the practical constraints of the evaluation context.

Donaldson suggests that one of the best examples to date of program theory–driven evaluation science in action is embodied in the Centers for Disease Control's (CDC) six-step Program Evaluation Framework (1999). He argues that this framework is not only conceptually well developed and instructive for evaluation practitioners, but also has been widely adopted for evaluating federally funded public health programs throughout the United States. The CDC framework begins to unpack the more concise three-step PT-DES model and offers more details to help guide practitioners:

1. *Engage stakeholders*—Those involved, those affected, primary intended users
2. *Describe the program*—Need, expected effects, activities, resources, stage, context, logic model
3. *Focus the evaluation design*—Purpose, users, uses, questions, methods, agreements
4. *Gather credible evidence*—Indicators, sources, quality, quantity, logistics
5. *Justify conclusions*—Standards, analysis and synthesis, interpretation, judgment, recommendations
6. *Ensure use and share lessons learned*—Design, preparation, feedback, follow-up, dissemination

The primary focus of PT-DES is on the development of program theory and evaluation questions. As a result, PT-DES is arguably method neutral. That is, the focus on program theory often creates a superordinate goal that helps evaluators move beyond the debates about which methods are superior to use in evaluation practice (Donaldson, forthcoming; Donaldson and Christie, 2005; Donaldson and Scriven, 2003). From this contingency point of view, it is believed that quantitative, qualitative, and mixed method designs are neither superior nor applicable in every evaluation context (Chen, 1997). Whether an evaluator uses case studies, observational methods, structured or unstructured interviews, online or telephone survey research, a quasi-experiment, or a randomized experimental trial to answer the key evaluation questions is dependent on discussions with relevant stakeholders about what would constitute credible evidence in this context and what is feasible given the practical and financial constraints.

Jean A. King. King is concerned with designing and implementing evaluations in a collaborative manner with stakeholders for the purpose of increasing the likelihood that the information generated from the evaluation will be used. This collaboration involves stakeholder participation throughout the evaluation process. Her theoretical approach, *interactive evaluation practice* (IEP), emphasizes participation, use, capacity building, and the "interpersonal factor" (King and Stevahn, 2005).

King describes the IEP framework as "the intentional act of engaging people in making decisions, taking action, and reflecting while conducting an evaluation study" (King and Stevahn, 2005). At its core, IEP is a participatory process. King (1998) argues that for a participatory evaluation to succeed, several conditions must be met. There must be an accepting power structure; shared meaning of experiences among participants, volunteers, and leaders; a great degree of interpersonal and organizational trust; enough time; and enough resources. An accepting power structure, King explains, is one that is open and willing to engage in the evaluation process and to use evaluative information to improve programs. For the evaluation to be successful, King underscores the importance of communication and discussion among stakeholders in creating shared meaning. She maintains that this process promotes interest in formulating methods of inquiry and collecting and interpreting data. The IEP evaluator also needs to identify and foster leaders during the evaluation process. Leaders, King argues, are needed to attract or recruit people to the evaluation process. They should be eager to learn and facilitate the evaluation process and "willing to stay the course when things go wrong" (King, 1998, p. 64). According to King, trust is a necessary condition for a successful participatory evaluation, and she urges evaluators to pay close attention to the interpersonal dynamics occurring during evaluations. She describes an evaluation without effective interpersonal interaction as "a machine without proper lubrication" (King and Stevahn, 2005).

The IEP evaluator has three primary roles: decision maker, actor, and reflective practitioner. As a decision maker, the evaluator is compelled to make decisions to facilitate the progress of the evaluation. Thus, the evaluator herself does not make crucial decisions about the program (that is, formative changes); rather, she makes decisions that propel the evaluation forward. As an actor, King explains, the evaluator participates in the evaluation process—which she describes as a "theatrical event"—as a "performer." That is, evaluators must see themselves as just one, albeit an important one, of many players in the evaluation process. The role of the evaluator, then, as a principal player, is that of a leader, a manager, and a "wise counselor." With her experience and expertise, the evaluator, as a reflective practitioner, also helps guide and assess evaluation progress. These three evaluator roles emphasize and reinforce the importance of the "personal factor" (Patton, 1997) when conducting evaluations.

Most recently, King has become more attentive to building evaluation capacity through participation as a means for ensuring ongoing evaluation use (King, 2002). This is foreshadowed in the work referenced here. The rationale for capacity building is that adults learn best by constructing personal meaning from their practice and can learn well in settings where they value both the task to be completed—in this case, the work of the school—and their collegial relationships (King and Stevahn, 2002). In addition to grounding in utilization focused evaluation, the origins of evaluation capacity building include the multiple traditions of action research (King and Lonnquist, 1994) and participatory evaluation and the concepts of organizational learning and professional community. In a grounded ECB framework, King and Volkov (2005) identify three areas of focus: (1) organizational context, including internal and external factors; (2) resources, including access to evaluation resources and sources of support for evaluation in the organization; and (3) structures, including an oversight mechanism, a formal ECB plan, core ECB principles in policies and procedures, infrastructure to support the evaluation process, purposeful socialization, and a peer learning structure.

Conclusion

In this chapter, we provide an argument for inviting Greene, Henry, Donaldson, and King to participate in an academic exercise that is intended to bring evaluation theories to life. We briefly summarize the main thrust of each of the theorists' models, with the intent of providing a general understanding of their approaches. This summary also serves as a frame for understanding the subsequent four chapters, in which each theorist describes how he or she would evaluate the Bunche–Da Vinci case presented in Chapter One.

What is exciting about the theorists' chapters is that each describes what they would actually do when designing an evaluation for this case. Evaluation theory literature largely addresses practice in the abstract. That is, theorists often argue what they believe to be the primary purpose of evaluation and how that purpose should shape the evaluation process. There is, of course, discussion of the principal components of the approach, but often these discussions are more conceptual. And this is understandable. There are many restrictions (such as page length) placed on authors when publishing manuscripts in journals and book chapters, the primary outlet for our theories. Thus, theorists are more or less mandated to discuss the defining features of their model, explaining what makes their approach unique. Consider, for example, House's earlier writings on social justice and evaluation. He spoke prolifically of inclusion and argued for increased participation of underrepresented groups in the evaluation process. He forced us to acknowledge that evaluation does in fact determine who gets what, and thus the need to represent all relevant stakeholders (most important, those who typically do not have a voice in our society) in the evaluation process equally. Yet it was difficult to imagine from these writings what House would actually do, step-by-step, when evaluating, for instance, a statewide education initiative.

In this chapter, we do not present a how-to description of theorists' approaches, in part because it is rare for theorists to publish such portrayals of their models. Instead, most theorists publish frameworks for action that describe the general approach the theorist espouses. This is because, by and large, evaluation designs and the implementation of these designs must be tailored to fit the specific program context. The particularities introduced by program context makes a one-size-fits all—it can work anywhere at any time—approach to evaluation relatively suspect. Thus, it is arguably more appropriate to present practical theories as general frameworks for actions that are meant to be adapted by and to circumstance. The how-to description, however, is of great interest to evaluators, as it helps bring color to some of the seemingly gray elements of a general framework. With this volume, the editors hope to introduce a bit of color to the theoretical landscape by presenting descriptions, written by the theorists themselves, of how to use their models in a specific program context.

References

Alkin, M. C., and Christie, C. A. "An Evaluation Theory Tree." In M. C. Alkin (ed.), *Evaluation Roots.* Thousand Oaks, Calif.: Sage, 2004.

Alkin, M. C., and House, E. "Evaluation of Programs." In M. C. Alkin (ed.), *Encyclopedia of Educational Research.* (6th ed.) Old Tappan, N.J.: Macmillan, 1992.

American Evaluation Association. "Guiding Principles for Evaluators." In W. R. Shadish, D. L. Newman, M. A. Scheirer, and C. Wye (eds.), *Guiding Principles for Evaluators.* New Directions for Program Evaluation, no. 34. San Francisco: Jossey-Bass, 1995.

Chen, H. "Applying Mixed Methods Under the Framework of Theory Driven Evaluations." In J. C. Greene and V. J. Caracelli (eds.), *Advances in Mixed-Method Evaluation: The Challenges and Benefits of Integrating Diverse Paradigms.* New Directions for Evaluation, no. 74. San Francisco: Jossey-Bass, 1997.

Chen, H. T. *Theory–Driven Evaluations.* Thousand Oaks, Calif.: Sage, 1990.

Cousins, J. B., and Whitmore, E. "Framing Participatory Evaluation." In E. Whitmore (ed.), *Understanding and Practicing Participatory Evaluation: New Directions for Evaluation.* New Directions in Evaluation, no. 80. San Francisco: Jossey-Bass, 1998.

Donaldson, S. I. "Overcoming Our Negative Reputation: Evaluation Becomes Known as a Helping Profession." *American Journal of Evaluation,* 2001, *22,* 355–361.

Donaldson, S. I. "Theory–Driven Program Evaluation in the New Millennium." In S. Donaldson and M. Scriven (eds.), *Evaluating Social Programs and Problems: Visions for the New Millennium.* Mahwah, N.J.: Erlbaum, 2003.

Donaldson, S. I. *Program Theory–Driven Evaluation Science: Strategies and Applications.* Mahwah, N.J.: Erlbaum forthcoming.

Donaldson, S. I. , and Christie, C. A. "The 2004 Claremont Debate: Lipsey vs. Scriven. Determining Causality in Program Evaluation and Applied Research: Should Experimental Evidence Be the Gold Standard?" *Journal of Multidisciplinary Evaluation,* 2005.

Donaldson, S. I., and Lipsey, M. W. "Roles for Theory in Evaluation Practice." In I. Shaw, J. Greene, and M. Mark (eds.), *Handbook of Evaluation.* Thousand Oaks, Calif.: Sage, forthcoming.

Donaldson, S. I., and Scriven, M. "Diverse Visions for Evaluation in the New Millennium: Should We Integrate or Embrace Diversity?" In S. I. Donaldson and M. Scriven (eds.), *Evaluating Social Programs and Problems: Visions for the New Millennium.* Mahwah, N.J.: Erlbaum, 2003.

Fetterman, D. M. *Foundations of Empowerment Evaluation.* Thousand Oaks, Calif.: Sage, 2001.

Fitzpatrick, J. L., Sanders, J. R., and Worthen, B. R. *Program Evaluation: Alternative Approaches and Practical Guidelines.* (3rd ed.) Needham Heights, Mass.: Allyn and Bacon, 2003.

Greene, J. G. "Challenges in Practicing Deliberative Democratic Evaluation." In R. R. Goetz, B. H. McFarland, and K. V. Ross (eds.), *What the Oregon Health Plan Can Teach*

Us About Managed Mental Health Care. New Directions for Mental Health Services, no. 85. San Francisco: Jossey-Bass, 2000.

Greene, J. G., and Caracelli, V. J. "Defining and Describing the Paradigm Issues in Mixed-Method Evaluation." In J. C. Greene and V. J. Caracelli (eds.), *Advances in Mixed-Method Evaluation: The Challenges and Benefits of Integrating Diverse Paradigms.* New Directions for Evaluation, no. 74. San Francisco: Jossey-Bass, 1997.

Henry, G. T. *Graphing Data: Techniques for Display and Analysis.* Thousand Oaks, Calif.: Sage, 1995.

Henry, G. T. "Does the Public Have a Role in Evaluation? Surveys and Democratic Discourse." In M. Braverman and J. K. Slater (eds.), *Advances in Survey Research.* New Directions for Evaluation, no. 70. San Francisco: Jossey-Bass, 1996.

House, E., and Howe, K. "Deliberative Democratic Evaluation." In R. R. Goetz, B. H. McFarland, and K. V. Ross (eds.), *What the Oregon Health Plan Can Teach Us About Managed Mental Health Care.* New Directions for Mental Health Services, no. 85. San Francisco: Jossey-Bass, 2000.

Joint Committee on Standards for Educational Evaluation. *The Program Evaluation Standards.* Thousand Oaks, Calif.: Sage, 1994.

Julnes, G. "Context-Confirmatory Methods for Supporting Disciplined Induction in Post-positivist Inquiry." Paper presented at the annual meeting of the American Evaluation Association, Vancouver, Canada, 1995.

King, J. A. "Making Sense of Participatory Evaluation Practice." In E. Whitmore (ed.), *Understanding and Practicing Participatory Evaluation: New Directions for Evaluation.* New Directions for Evaluation, no. 80. San Francisco: Jossey-Bass, 1998.

King, J. A. "Building Evaluation Capacity in a School District." In D. W. Compton, M. Baizerman, and S. H. Stockdill (eds.), *The Art, Craft, and Science of Evaluation Capacity Building.* New Directions for Evaluation, no. 93. San Francisco: Jossey-Bass, 2002.

King, J. A., and Lonnquist, M. P. *Learning from the Literature: Fifty Years of Action Research.* Madison, Wis.: Center for the Organization and Restructuring of Schools, 1994.

King, J. A., and Stevahn, L. "Three Frameworks for Considering Evaluator Role." In K. E. Ryan and T. A. Schwandt (eds.), *Exploring Evaluator Role and Identity.* Greenwich, Conn.: Information Age Publishing, 2002.

King, J. A., and Stevahn, L. "Interactive Evaluation Practice: Managing the Interpersonal Dynamics of Program Evaluation." Unpublished manuscript, 2005.

King, J. A., and Volkov, B. "A Grounded Framework for Evaluation Capacity Building." Unpublished manuscript, University of Minnesota, 2005.

Mark, M. M., Henry, G. T., and Julnes, G. "A Realist Theory of Evaluation Practice." In G. T. Henry, G. Julnes, and M. M. Mark (eds.), *Realist Evaluation: An Emerging Theory in Support of Practice.* New Directions for Evaluation, no. 78. San Francisco: Jossey-Bass, 1998.

Mark, M. M., Henry, G. T., and Julnes G. *Evaluation: An Integrated Framework for Understanding, Guiding, and Improving Public and Non-Profit Policies and Programs.* San Francisco: Jossey-Bass, 2000.

Patton, M. Q. *Utilization-Focused Evaluation: The New Century Text.* (3rd ed.) Thousand Oaks, Calif.: Sage, 1997.

Preskill, H., and Torres, R. T. *Evaluative Inquiry for Learning in Organizations.* Thousand Oaks, Calif.: Sage, 1999.

Rossi, P. H., and Freeman, H. E. *Evaluation: A Systematic Approach.* (5th ed.) Thousand Oaks, Calif.: Sage, 1993.

Shadish, W. R., Cook, T. D., and Leviton, L. C. *Foundations of Program Evaluation: Theories of Practice.* Thousand Oaks, Calif.: Sage, 1991.

Stake, R. E. "Program Evaluation, Particularly Responsive Evaluation." In W. B. Dockrell and D. Hamilton (eds.), *Rethinking Educational Research.* London: Hodder and Stoughton, 1980.

Stake, R. E. "Program Evaluation, Particularly Responsive Evaluation." In G. F. Madus, M. S. Scriven, and D. L. Stufflebeam (eds.), *Evaluation Models: Viewpoints on Educational and Human Services Evaluation.* Norwood, Mass.: Kluwer-Nijhoff, 1987.

Stake, R. E. "Stake and Responsive Evaluation." In M. C. Alkin (ed.), *Evaluation Roots.* Thousand Oaks, Calif.: Sage, 2004.

Tukey, J. W. *Exploratory Data Analysis.* Reading, Mass.: Addison-Wesley, 1977.

Weiss, C. H. *Evaluation: Methods for Studying Programs and Policies.* (2nd ed.) Upper Saddle River, N.J.: Prentice Hall, 1998.

CHRISTINA A. CHRISTIE is an assistant professor and associate director of the Institute of Organizational and Program Evaluation Research at Claremont Graduate University.

TAREK AZZAM is a doctoral student in the Social Research Methods Division in the Graduate School of Education and Information Studies at the University of California, Los Angeles.

3

As illustrated in the Bunche–Da Vinci context, a value-engaged approach to evaluation emphasizes responsiveness to the particularities of the context, inclusion of and engagement with multiple stakeholder perspectives and experiences, and attention to the social and relational dimensions of evaluation practice.

A Value-Engaged Approach for Evaluating the Bunche–Da Vinci Learning Academy

Jennifer C. Greene

A value-engaged approach to program evaluation blends elements of responsiveness (Abma and Stake, 2001; Stake, 1987, 2004) with an active engagement with values that are drawn principally from democratic and culturally responsive traditions in evaluation (Hood, 1999; House and Howe, 1999; MacDonald, 1977). These values include commitments to contextuality, inclusion, learning, diversity, and the public good (as elaborated later in this chapter). Because value-engaged evaluation is fundamentally responsive to the particular character of an evaluation context and the programmatic and policy issues that are present in that context, it is not possible to develop an a priori or preordinate (Stake, 1987) evaluation design using this approach. Rather, the evaluation design evolves as the evaluator comes to know the context, its people, and its joys and troubles. In fact, considerable effort is allocated in this evaluation approach to the front-end aspects of evaluation practice: learning about the context and the program to be evaluated, developing appropriate relationships with key stakeholders in the setting, understanding in some depth the critical issues to be addressed, identifying priority evaluation questions, and determining criteria for making judgments of program quality. Only after all of these facets of evaluation practice are engaged can an evaluation design be developed and implemented. In these critical ways, the evaluation process becomes integrally interwoven with the context.

Therefore, this narrative of a value-engaged approach to evaluating the Bunche–Da Vinci Learning Academy concentrates on envisioning these front-end aspects of evaluation in this context. Assumptions will also be made along the way to enable a more complete story to be told.

NEW DIRECTIONS FOR EVALUATION, no. 106, Summer 2005 © Wiley Periodicals, Inc.

Developing an Understanding of the Context and the Program to Be Evaluated

TO:	Mary García, Principal, Bunche–Da Vinci Learning Academy,
	<marygarcia@majorcity.K12.edu>
FROM:	Jennifer Greene, UIUC <jcgreene@uiuc.edu>
DATE:	March 15, 2004
RE:	Possible Evaluation Project
CC:	Douglas Chase, District Superintendent
	<douglaschase@majorcity.K12.edu>

Dear Ms. García:

Thank you very much for inviting me to develop a proposal for evaluating the Bunche–Da Vinci Learning Academy. I am keenly committed to strong schools for *all* of our nation's children and thus am eager to work with you and others at your school on this important evaluation project.

I would like to learn more about your school and its current programs, teachers, students, and families, as well as the interesting and unique relationship the school has with the Da Vinci Learning Corporation. This will enable me to develop an evaluation plan that can yield the kinds of information likely to be meaningful and useful to your school community at this time.

For this purpose, I am hoping that I can visit Bunche–Da Vinci several times this spring and review relevant materials (for example, annual reports and previous evaluation studies), talk with various members of your community, as well as simply spend some time at your school. While there, I can also learn more about the kinds of evaluation priorities that various members of your school community have. I will follow up this email with a phone call to pursue this idea further and hopefully identify particular days for my visits.

I am looking forward to meeting you. Thank you for your consideration.

The Bunche–Da Vinci Community

The Bunche–Da Vinci elementary school community appears to be similar to many urban school communities today in terms of demographics that overrepresent racial and ethnic minorities in the United States, a history of inadequate educational resources, and persistent challenges of effective teaching and learning. Specifically, the Bunche–Da Vinci school community is located in a geographical buffer zone between an industrial sector of an urban port city and a historically working-class suburb, known for its poverty, crime, and racial tensions. The school mostly draws students from economically marginal families in these neighboring communities—at this time predominantly (nearly 80 percent) Latino with an additional 17 percent African American out of a total school population of about twelve hundred. In fact, the school's Latino enrollment has increased by 50 percent in the past ten years, with concomitant decreases in all other groups. Nearly two-thirds of the school's students speak English as a second language; for nearly all of these students, their first language is Spanish. Year-to-year student turnover at Bunche–Da Vinci is considerable, even though many parents express satisfaction with the school and most students appear to like being at this school.

A very important first step in developing an evaluation plan for the Bunche–Da Vinci Learning Academy is to better understand the particular characteristics and diversities of this school community. In fact, given that this school community shares many characteristics with other urban school communities of today, it is especially important *not* to make assumptions about this particular context based on urban stereotypes. Such assumptions might include, for example, that Bunche–Da Vinci parents are at best modestly involved in their children's education or that drugs dominate the community's economic exchanges. Learning about this particular school community—its uniqueness, its complexities, and its continuing and dynamic evolution—is fundamental to developing an evaluation plan that holds promise of generating meaningful information. And for this purpose, it may well be that the evaluator in this context needs to enlist, as evaluation team members or as consultants to the evaluation, people who share substantial sociocultural and political history with members of the Bunche–Da Vinci school community. Key informants within the school can help in learning about this community, but that will probably not be enough.

TO:	Estella Marquez <emarquez@uiuc.edu>,
	Hashid Robinson <hjr3@uiuc.edu [graduate students]
FROM:	Jennifer Greene <jcgreene@uiuc.edu>
DATE:	March 20, 2004
RE:	An evaluation opportunity

Hi, Estella and Hashid,

I am beginning to get involved in an interesting evaluation project in an urban elementary school community. The school is involved in a unique partnership with a nonprofit company that offers a whole-school program designed specifically for low-performing schools. The school population presently is nearly 80 percent Latino and 17 percent African American. I believe that it will be vital to have evaluation team members who can understand the social, cultural, and political strands of this context better than I can. I thought of the two of you as potential team members given your past experiences as teachers in similar communities and your fluency in Spanish.

Might you be interested in joining me in this project? I believe each of you can add another ten hours per week of paid work. The project is likely to last two years, beginning this summer. Can we discuss this at the end of our NSF [National Science Foundation] project meeting next Tuesday? Please let me know meanwhile of your potential interest in this project.

Thanks.

Jennifer

The Da Vinci School Reform Program

Three years ago, the Bunche Academy was chosen by its district to join in partnership with the Da Vinci Learning Corporation to embark on an ambitious whole-school reform initiative, especially designed by the corporation for low-performing schools. Uniquely, the Da Vinci Learning Corporation has primary control over the school's programs and full control over its budget, but the school remains part of the school district. Important mandated features of the Da Vinci school reform program include the following:

An extended school day and extended school year

Specified maximum student-teacher ratios of 20:1 for grades K to 3 and 35:1 for grades 4 and 5 (except during reading, when the required ratio is also 20:1)

Placement of students in reading and mathematics groups by ability level, regardless of grade level, so first and fifth graders could be in the same group

A full curriculum: reading, mathematics, language arts, science, social studies, music, art, physical education, modern foreign languages, and values education

Integration of special services (like Title I) into the regular classroom, except for a pull-out Structured English Immersion program for English language learners whose English fluency requires such instruction

Extensive technological equipment in the school, including laptops and personal digital assistants for all teachers and ready computer access for all students

Specialized achievement assessments, conducted using the computer, beginning at second grade

The Bunche–Da Vinci Learning Academy

As noted, the Da Vinci Learning Corporation requires that its intervention program be implemented as prescribed, and the corporation has full control over the school's budget. In this unique public-corporate partnership, however, the school remains part of the school district. Just what this means is not entirely clear.

Available information does suggest that the partnership has experienced tensions and challenges since its inception three years ago, despite the committed leadership of the school's principal, Mary García, and the broader support of the district administration. Notably, teachers, many of whom are quite young and about one-fourth of whom have emergency credentials, report considerable stress and pressure to work long hours implementing a curriculum that feels foreign or "imported," much of which does not "count" under the federal No Child Left Behind legislation. For example, the Da Vinci reading program is at variance with the state-adopted program, and the technology demands of the curriculum seem to take valuable time away from more basic teaching and learning. Some teacher comments even suggest that they may feel that their professional judgment is undermined by the inflexible structure and demands of the Da Vinci program. Teacher turnover at the school is high. Parent participation in school governance and school activities is minimal. And student achievement scores on state-mandated language arts tests, while showing small gains in year 2 of the partnership, dropped to levels that were below the school's scores at the outset of the partnership—both overall and for all subgroups. Only about one-fourth of the school's population demonstrates proficiency on this language arts test. (Student performance on state tests in other subjects may well be similar.) This is so even though student performance on the Da Vinci standardized tests has demonstrated consistent improvement over the past three years. In addition, parents and students report being happy with the school, which is not congruent with the fact that large numbers of students leave the school each year.

Just What Is Being Evaluated?

As with developing an understanding of the broader school community, a more complete understanding of the Da Vinci program and its implementation in the Bunche–Da Vinci Learning Academy is a critical initial step in a value-engaged approach to evaluation. Only with such an understanding can the evaluation be anchored in the concerns and issues (Guba and Lincoln, 1989; Stake, 2004) of important priority in this context. Identification of the evaluand, or just what is being evaluated, is not assumed in this evaluation approach, but rather is a matter of discussion among as many stakeholder groups as possible in this front-end part of the evaluation. The evaluator contributes to this discussion her or his expertise and perspectives, including ideas from relevant research literature. In this context, for example, the perspectives of theory-oriented evaluation may be relevant and useful, as they could catalyze an explication of the conceptual rationales underlying the Da Vinci program *and* the Bunche–Da Vinci partnership, and thereby enable examination and critique of these rationales as part of the evaluation.

Notably, this particular context features the Da Vinci Learning Corporation's educational intervention for low-performing schools, *and* it features the unique public-corporate partnership. Both are viable candidates for evaluation, among perhaps others. And both potentially engage very important educational issues of all times—issues of pedagogy, curriculum, differentiation, and individualization—as well as issues more specific to these times: how and what to teach English language learners, the contributions of technology to learning, and teacher professionalism, as well as the educational effectiveness of state-imposed standards, accountability requirements, and the privatization of public education. Two questions are addressed in this front-end evaluative process: Which issues matter in this context? and What particular form do they take?

Spending valuable evaluative time on developing an accurate and thoughtful understanding of what is being evaluated in this particular context anchors the development of meaningful and potentially useful evaluation questions. It also reflects some of the value commitments of this value-engaged evaluation approach, specifically:

A commitment to *contextuality*, to understanding the character of the program (and/or institutional structure, like a partnership) to be evaluated in its particular and unique context

A commitment to *inclusion* of all legitimate stakeholder views and perspectives on the issues in the evaluation, with special efforts to include the more marginalized people in the context (House and Howe, 1999)—perhaps, in this particular school community, discouraged teachers and transient families

In the value-engaged evaluation plan to be developed in this context, considerable space is allocated to this description of just what is being evaluated and its distinctive characteristics. This description provides the contextual anchor and justification for the evaluation plan that is developed.

Identifying the Key Evaluation Questions

TO: Mary García, Principal, Bunche-Da Vinci Learning Academy,
                <marygarcia@majorcity.K12.edu>
FROM: Jennifer Greene, UIUC <jcgreene@uiuc.edu>
DATE: April 25, 2004
RE: Evaluation Priorities

Hi, Mary,

Thanks very much for all of your assistance in hosting our visits to the Bunche–Da Vinci Learning Academy this past month–arranging times to talk with teachers and parents, providing copies of relevant materials, helping us make connections to Dr. Richardson at the Da Vinci Learning Corporation and to Doug [the superintendent], as well as spending so much time with us yourself. We wish more parents had come to the meeting we held in El Centro de Comunidad Latina, but we value the ideas of the six parents who did show up. We will continue trying various ideas to connect with your parent communities. Estella, Hashid, and I remain very excited about working with your school community on this evaluation project.

We want to confirm the preliminary evaluation priorities that emerged from the discussion at your faculty meeting last Thursday. As you recall, we brought to that meeting key evaluation priorities identified during our conversations in and around your school over the past month and from our review of relevant documents, and we invited further faculty comment on these priorities during the meeting. Based on all of these conversations and analyses, the most important clusters of evaluation priorities at this time concern the following issues:

- Teachers at Bunche–Da Vinci feel overloaded with the demands of the curriculum, the long hours, and the extra courses they need to take to meet credentialing requirements. Teachers also feel underappreciated as professionals—by both the district and the parents of their students. Teachers therefore don't stay at Da Vinci if they have another opportunity. With constant teacher turnover, it is hard to develop and sustain a sense of community in the school.

- The Da Vinci curriculum is being questioned by teachers and parents alike for its relevance to their children and for its power to enable meaningful learning by the children, especially learning in language arts and mathematics (the core subjects of state tests). Of special concern in the curriculum are the technology components, including computer-aided instruction, the foreign language instruction, and the values instruction. "What values?" wonder some parents.

- Teachers and parents are further especially concerned about the relevance and effectiveness of the curriculum in meeting the needs of English language learners and students with special needs.

- Many in the school community express concerns about the integration of most special services into the regular classroom and curriculum, notably Title I and special education. Integration is an ideal, but without appropriate staff in each classroom, these children may not be getting the specialized services they need.

- The school and district personnel wonder why so many families don't stay at Da Vinci, but rather transfer after just one or two years. "Is it problems in cohesion and sense of belonging within the school community?" they wonder.

- Da Vinci Corporation personnel are most committed to raising the test scores of participating students on both their own assessments and the state tests as well. School personnel are equally concerned about student test performance, especially on state tests.

- Administrators in the school and district are concerned that the school leadership does not have the authority to make changes in the Da Vinci program as might be needed, given the particular characteristics of the school's population. Budget authority should be fully shared, they think.

We will use these evaluation priorities as the basis for developing our key evaluation questions and our evaluation plan, recognizing, of course, that other issues may emerge over the coming year as the plan is implemented. We will be drafting this plan over the coming few weeks and will share it with you when available.

Also, attached please find a draft of our description of the Bunche–Da Vinci Learning Academy and its surrounding communities. When you get the chance, we would welcome your feedback on this draft, especially its accuracy and completeness. We also intend to share this draft with several teachers and community members who have been involved in this school for many years and who also volunteered to provide feedback.

Thank you for your continuing cooperation.

Jennifer

The major purpose of evaluation in a value-engaged approach is to aug-ment our understanding of the quality and effectiveness of the evaluand in the particular context at hand. This is a fundamentally educative vision for evaluation (Cronbach and Associates, 1980). Furthermore, this requires that the evaluation include assessments of the program as implemented and experienced, as well as assessments of what important differences the pro-gram has made in the lives of its participants. Moreover, in a value-engaged approach, evaluation questions attend specifically to the interests of people traditionally underserved in our country, including racial and ethnic minorities, low-income people, immigrants, and people with disabilities. The interests of the majority are not excluded in this evaluation approach; rather, the interests of the minorities are specifically included. These frames for evaluation questions reflect additional value commitments underlying this value-engaged approach to evaluation:

A commitment to *learning* in and through evaluation, to contribute to bet-ter understanding of how well the program being evaluated meets impor-tant needs and interests of participants in the particular setting at hand (in addition to how well participants perform in the program)
A commitment to *engaging with difference and diversity* as manifested in the context at hand, to assess how well the program being evaluated meets the particular needs and interests of people traditionally underserved, which may well be most of the children and families in the Bunche–Da Vinci context

Given these frames for identifying evaluation questions and given the evaluation priorities identified by Bunche–Da Vinci stakeholders, the key eval-uation questions to be addressed in this value-engaged evaluation of the Bunche–Da Vinci Learning Academy are (provisionally) the following:

Overall Question
In what ways and to what extent does the educational program offered at the Bunche–Da Vinci Learning Academy meet the important educational needs of the children and families served by this school, in particular the distinctive needs of English language learners, children from racial and ethnic minority groups, children from low-income families, and children with special needs? And in what ways and to what extent does the struc-ture of the partnership support this primary educational mission?

Subquestions
1. What is the *quality of the educational program* offered at Bunche–Da Vinci Learning Academy for this particular community of children and families?
   • What are the particular contributions of the technology, foreign lan-guage, and values components of the program to the meaningfulness of children's educational experiences and learning, again for all chil-dren in the school and for children with distinctive learning needs?

- How well are the particular needs of children eligible for Title I, special education, and English language instruction being met by the in-class model of integrated services?
- How well prepared and supported are Bunche–Da Vinci teachers to implement the Da Vinci program with high educational quality in this school?
- What are parent and guardian perceptions of the school's educational quality, and how do these perceptions relate to parental commitment to the school?

2. To what extent and in what ways are the children at the Bunche-Da Vinci Learning Academy *attaining meaningful and valued educational outcomes?*
   - What accounts for the discrepancy in scores on the Da Vinci tests and the state tests in recent years, overall and for various subgroups of children?
   - To what extent does the Da Vinci program provide sufficient and appropriate instructional time and practice on basic skills in language arts and math for all children in the school, especially those with histories of low achievement? And how does this relate to children's mastery and achievement in these core subject areas?

Establishing the Criteria for Making Judgments of Program Quality

A final front-end facet of evaluation concerns the criteria to be used to make judgments of program quality. In a value-engaged approach to evaluation, these criteria are not assumed but rather are established through discussions with diverse stakeholders, in tandem with relevant external perspectives contributed by the evaluator. Moreover, discussions about quality criteria are especially important for stakeholder inclusion, as criteria can and should engage and reflect the multiplicity of cherished values and ideals in the context at hand.

TO:	Mary García, Principal, Bunche–Da Vinci Learning Academy
	<marygarcia@majorcity.K12.edu>,
	Sandra Martin <sandramartin@majorcity.K12.edu>
FROM:	Jennifer Greene, UIUC <jcgreene@uiuc.edu>
DATE:	May 10, 2004
RE:	What matters for program quality

Hello, Mary and Sandra [lead teacher contact for the evaluation],

We have completed our analysis of what various members of your school community said when we asked them, "What matters to you most in an educational program for children at this school? And how would you know that the program in this school is a good one?" We asked these kinds of questions in all of our various conversations and meetings at Bunche–Da Vinci last month.

Attached to this email please find our draft of these results. We are hoping you can share this draft among the Bunche–Da Vinci staff and gather any feedback they may have. We ourselves will work through two community groups with whom we have made connections to further engage parents and families in this process. We are hoping to refine this list by the end of the month, so if we can have your feedback by May 26, that would be great.
Thanks.
Jennifer

Criteria for judging educational quality in this context are complicated by the presence of the Da Vinci program, which likely has its own criteria of quality (which are not yet known), and by the diversity of program stakeholders. A draft set of general criteria envisioned as possible in this context includes the following:

The curriculum and the pedagogy are of high quality, based on relevant theory and research (for example, research on effective teachers of minority children) and based on the perspectives and experiences of the Bunche–Da Vinci staff and families.

The curriculum and pedagogy offer relevant and valuable approaches to learning for all of Bunche–Da Vinci's particular population of students.

The curricular program and its assessments are well aligned with state standards in all subject areas, especially language arts and mathematics.

All students at Bunche–Da Vinci have meaningful and positive learning experiences and demonstrate strong and consistent mastery of valued skills and knowledge, especially in language arts and mathematics, as assessed by Da Vinci tests, state tests, and teacher judgment, among other possible achievement measures. On the state tests, student performance should be high enough each year to ensure that the school is not placed on the state's "watch list."

The Bunche–Da Vinci Learning Academy community holds high expectations for all students' learning, values and affirms the worth of all community members, and demonstrates caring and support for all community members; *and* members of this community are happy and satisfied to belong to it.

The Bunche–Da Vinci partnership structure affirms and supports *public responsibility and authority* for the education of this community's children.

The last criterion in this list represents a final value commitment in value-engaged evaluation, specifically:

A commitment to engaging with issues related to the *public good* in an evaluative context, that is, issues related to civic responsibility, public policy priorities, democratic ideals, or in this context, vital public responsibilities for education

The Evaluation Design

The full evaluation plan for the Bunche–Da Vinci Learning Academy would have three parts. It would begin with a rich description of the program and its context (including relevant history), a clear statement of the primary evaluation purposes and audiences (including the various stakeholder interests in the evaluation), and a presentation of the key evaluation questions and critical criteria for judging quality. The process for establishing these front-end components of the evaluation plan was described and illustrated above. Second, the more technical evaluation design section of the plan would specify the overall inquiry design to be used, along with the data-gathering methods and samples, analysis procedures, technical quality considerations, informed-consent procedures, and reporting plans. Finally, the third section of the plan would present information on evaluation management, staffing, and budget (not included in this narrative). Below, highlights of a likely evaluation design from the second part of the plan are offered as illustrations of this approach in practice. Specifically, the overall design, methods and samples, and reporting sections are presented. Because this evaluation approach is fundamentally responsive, all aspects of the design could be changed as appropriate given evolving issues and concerns in the setting.

Overall Design. This evaluation of the Bunche–Da Vinci Learning Academy will be designed as an interpretive case study with multiple and mixed methods implemented for purposes of understanding selected phenomena more comprehensively and with greater insight and value consciousness (Greene, Benjamin, and Goodyear, 2001). This case study seeks to develop an in-depth understanding of the quality and experiential meaningfulness of the Da Vinci program as specifically implemented in the Bunch–Da Vinci Learning Academy.

Methods and Samples. The methods and samples for this case study emphasize assessments of the quality of the program experience for students and teachers in the school, but also include analyses of relevant achievement test data.

Curriculum Review. The complete Da Vinci curriculum will be reviewed by approximately five experts in curriculum and the teaching of children like those in the Bunche–Da Vinci school population. The review will concentrate on addressing the questions of curricular quality and especially of curricular fit to the Bunche–Da Vinci school population, using carefully identified criteria. These criteria are likely to include elements representing the Da Vinci program's underlying theoretical rationale, as well as factors drawn from the research literature. The principal developers of this program at the Da Vinci Learning Corporation will be interviewed as part of this curriculum review process, specifically to learn about the program's rationale or theory from the perspective of the developers. The Da Vinci Learning Corporation will also participate in the identification of the expert reviewers.

Classroom and School Observations. One class at each grade level will be selected for regular observations by the evaluation team. Classes will be identified as "representative or typical" and will require teacher and parent consent. The observations will be made about once a week for about half of the school day during the months of October, November, February, March, and April, scheduled so that all components of the curriculum are observed multiple times. The observations will generate rich descriptions of the learning activities, interactions, and environments of these classrooms. Specific focuses for observations, as specified in the key evaluation questions, include the engagement and learning of different kinds of children in the various components of the curriculum (notably the computer, foreign language instruction, and values education); the character of the integrated in-class services provided to children eligible for Title I, English language instruction, and special education; and how the time allocated to language arts and mathematics instruction is used. Other observation focuses may well emerge during the course of the evaluation. A smaller set of observations of all classes within the Structured English Immersion program will also be conducted, both to describe this program as implemented and assess the quality of the learning experiences it is providing for English language learners.

In addition, the evaluation team will record field notes of unstructured observations conducted at other sites in the school, including the lunchroom and the playground. These field notes will contribute primarily to the descriptive portrait of the daily life in the school to be developed in the evaluation.

Teacher and Administrator Interviews. A purposive sample of about fifteen teachers will be individually interviewed. The sample will be selected to be collectively representative of the school's faculty, along dimensions of education, experience, longevity at the school, classroom or specialist assignment, race and ethnicity, and commitment to the school. Very new teachers and teachers new to the school will be excluded, as they are unlikely to provide information as rich as more experienced faculty. The interviews will gather teacher descriptions of their experiences with the Da Vinci curriculum in this school, their reflections on its value for the school's population of children, and their evaluations of their own challenges and successes in the program.

In addition, the school principal, the district superintendent, and other key administrators in the school and district (for example, the directors of curriculum, Title I, special education, and English as a Second Language) will also be individually interviewed to gather administrative views on the quality and effectiveness of the Da Vinci program as implemented in the Bunche Academy.

Information on Teacher Quality. With the consent of the teachers' union and the district and school administrators, the evaluation team will endeavor to secure group-level evaluative information about the Bunche–Da Vinci teaching staff over the past three years. Information about individual teachers will not be requested. Rather, a group-level profile of strengths and weaknesses will be sought. If access to this information is denied, the evaluation team will consult with the administration and faculty at Bunche–Da Vinci regarding other avenues to secure data on teaching quality.

Parent Interviews. Six group interviews of parents will be conducted. From five to ten parents will participate in each group interview. The groups will be formed primarily around the demographics of the school and will include (1) one group of Latino parents of children who have good English fluency, (2) one group of Latino parents of children in the Structured English Immersion classes, (3) one group of African American parents, (4) one group of parents of children in Title I, and (5) one group of parents of children in special education. The sixth group will comprise parents who have asserted some leadership or active involvement in the school. For all groups, parents will be sampled for representativeness, along criteria of age, gender, work and income status, longevity in the community, longevity in the Bunche–Da Vinci school, and number of children in the school. Child care, transportation, and food will be provided for all group interviews. In addition, interviews will be conducted in Spanish if the Spanish-speaking parents prefer this. The major focus of these interviews will be to gather parent descriptions of and evaluative reflections on their children's learning experiences in this school, as well as their own sense of connectedness and commitment to the school.

Test and Test Score Analysis. A full content analysis and comparison of the Da Vinci program tests, the state tests and standards, and teacher-developed assessments will be conducted by the evaluation team, with the consultation of two experts in psychometrics and additional content experts as needed (particularly for language arts and mathematics). In addition, student performance on all of these tests over the past four years, using the first year before the Da Vinci partnership as a baseline, will be analyzed by student subgroup and skill area. This analysis will endeavor to identify the specific areas of relative strength and weakness displayed by various subgroups of students, as well as patterns in performance over time, again for subgroups and specific skill areas.

A summary of methods as connected to evaluation questions is presented in Table 3.1.

Reporting

TO: Mary García, Principal, Bunche-Da Vinci Learning
               Academy
               <marygarcia@majorcity.K12.edu>
FROM: Jennifer Greene, UIUC <jcgreene@uiuc.edu>
DATE: June 5, 2004
RE: Scheduling time for evaluation reporting

Hi, Mary,

As always, thanks for all of your help, and Sandra's, too, in coordinating the feedback from your staff regarding the program quality criteria. And we

Table 3.1. Evaluation Questions and Methods

Evaluation Question	Curriculum Review	Classroom and School Observations	Teacher and Administrator Interviews	Summary of Group Data on Teacher Quality	Parent Group Interviews	Test and Test Score Analysis
What is the quality of the school's educational program for this particular community of children and families?	XX	XX	XX	XX	XX	
• What are the particular contributions of the technology, foreign language, and values components of the program to the meaningfulness of children's educational experiences and learning, again for all children in the school and for children with distinctive learning needs?	XX	XX	X		X	
• How well are the particular needs of children eligible for Title I, special education, and English language instruction being met by the in-class model of integrated services?	XX	XX	X		X	
• How well prepared and supported are Bunche-Da Vinci teachers to implement the Da Vinci program with high educational quality in this school?	X	XX	XX	XX		
• What are parent and guardian perceptions of the school's educational quality, and how do these perceptions relate to parental commitment to the school?			X		XX	

Evaluation Question	Curriculum Review	Classroom and School Observations	Teacher and Administrator Interviews	Summary of Group Data on Teacher Quality	Parent Group Interviews	Test and Test Score Analysis
To what extent and in what ways are the children at the Bunche-Da Vinci Learning Academy attaining meaningful and valued educational outcomes?	XX	X	XX		XX	XX
• What accounts for the discrepancy in scores on the Da Vinci tests and the state tests in recent years, overall, and for various subgroups of children?	XX					XX
• To what extent does the Da Vinci program provide sufficient and appropriate instructional time and practice on basic skills in language arts and math for all children in the school, especially those with histories of low achievement? And how does this relate to children's mastery and achievement in these core subject areas?	XX	XX	X		X	XX

Note: XX = Primary method for that evaluation question. X = Secondary method for that evaluation question.

appreciate the thoughtful input of the faculty and teaching aides regarding our evaluation methods and data to be gathered.

We are working now on the reporting section of our evaluation plan. Our desire is to provide periodic brief reports on the evaluation's progress first in writing and then in person, including time for questions, comments, and discussion. We believe that ongoing engagement in the evaluative issues being pursued, especially by your staff and interested parents, can enhance the potential power of the evaluation to be a meaningful and valuable learning activity. For example, teacher discussions of interim evaluation findings can offer them some time and a safe place for critical reflections on their own practice.

So, the question is, for this first year of the evaluation, can we reserve one of your faculty meetings for evaluation reporting and discussion in mid-November, one in early March, and then one in late May? We intend to schedule parallel meetings with district and parent groups at separate times and locations. Yet we also thought that it could be useful to have a joint public forum for all interested members of the Bunche–Da Vinci community to discuss *with one another* the emerging findings and continuing issues being engaged in the evaluation. Perhaps this could be scheduled for the March reporting time? We could organize a pasta and salad dinner for the occasion, and we would have interpreters there for the Spanish-speaking parents. And maybe there is another school event or festivity that could be coordinated with this evaluation forum?

Realizing the multiple demands on staff time, we understand that we may need to creatively generate some other ideas to find time for evaluation reporting and discussions of emerging findings. We are hoping, however, that some of these initial ideas are workable.

Looking forward to hearing from you.

Thanks.

Jennifer

As indicated in the above email to Mary García, every three to four months, the evaluation team will present written progress reports to the leadership of the Bunche–Da Vinci Learning Academy (principal and lead teachers), the district leadership (superintendent and identified others), interested parent and community groups, and designated representatives of the Da Vinci Learning Corporation. These reports will outline in brief, nontechnical form the major evaluation activities accomplished since the last progress report, highlights of recent evaluation findings available, and activities upcoming in the near future. The evaluation team will then schedule times to discuss the progress reports with various stakeholder groups, inviting and encouraging an ongoing dialogue about the issues being pursued. As possible, forums for discussion among multiple and diverse stakeholders will also be scheduled, at least once each year.

In addition, more formal and comprehensive evaluation reports, including presentations of all data collected, will be generated and disseminated on an annual basis for each of the two years of the evaluation. Audiences for these technical reports will include school and district leadership and the Da Vinci Learning Corporation. In addition, a nontechnical summary of the highlights of these annual reports will be prepared for wider dissemination to other teachers, parents, and interested community members in the Bunch–Da Vinci community. Resources permitting, a Spanish version of all progress and annual highlights reports will be prepared for the Spanish-speaking members of the community.

The Evaluation Process

A value-engaged approach to evaluation happens close-up, in and around the setting of the evaluand. There is no other way to develop an accurate and appreciative understanding of the unique characteristics of the evaluand in the particular context at hand. Moreover, a value-engaged approach to evaluation is fundamentally responsive to the issues and concerns of all legitimate stakeholder groups in that context. This again requires an on-site presence and an ear keenly tuned to the multiple and diverse rhythms of lived experiences in this particular community. A value-engaged approach is also fundamentally educative, aspiring to provide spaces and places for thoughtful, data-informed reflections on practice—in this case, on curricula, teaching, learning, and the distinctive educational needs of diverse kinds of children.

   With these characteristics, the value-engaged evaluator must attend not only to the substantive and methodological dimensions of the evaluation, but also its relational dimensions, to how the evaluator is present in the context at hand—in other words, to the process of conducting the evaluation, to evaluation itself as a moral and ethical practice (Schwandt, 2004). In the Bunche–Da Vinci context, these relational and practical dimensions of evaluation will be intentionally enacted in three principal ways. First, the evaluator will try to establish respectful, reciprocal, partnering relationships with all stakeholders in the Bunche–Da Vinci school community. Respect and reciprocity can be communicated, for example, by assuming that all stakeholders have something valuable to contribute to the evaluation and by listening well to each one (Greene, 2003). Second, the evaluation process will be an open and transparent one that invites participation by multiple stakeholders in all phases, but especially at the front end, when the evaluation agenda is being established, and at the back end, when interpretations of results and action implications are discussed. Most important in terms of participation is the inclusion of all legitimate stakeholder perspectives in the evaluation and anchoring of the evaluative work in the particularities of this context. Less important is actual stakeholder participation in the nitty-gritty activities of data gathering and analysis, although stakeholders would be welcome in these processes as well. And third, the value-engaged evaluator will seek opportunities for meaningful dialogues with stakeholders and especially opportunities for stakeholders to engage in dialogue with one another about their respective experiences and perspectives in the Bunche–Da Vinci Learning Academy (Abma, 2001). Although such opportunities may be rare, the value-engaged evaluator holds dialogue as a particularly valuable way in which relational respect, responsiveness, and especially learning can be enacted.

Meta-Evaluation

Finally, near the end of the two years of this evaluation project, a modest meta-evaluation will be commissioned for this value-engaged evaluation of the Bunche–Da Vinci Learning Academy. Two well-regarded evaluators will be contracted to evaluate this evaluation. One will be an evaluator who advocates responsiveness and learning in evaluation practice, and one will be an evaluator with a different evaluative philosophy and practical approach, perhaps more utilization oriented or theory based or emphasizing causal knowledge claims. Each meta-evaluator will be encouraged to evaluate this evaluation on the basis of (1) criteria intrinsic to this approach, (2) the widely accepted evaluation standards (utility, feasibility, propriety, accuracy), and (3) her or his own ideas about what constitutes "good" evaluation practice. On completion of their work, the meta-evaluators will be invited to two forums for presentation and discussion of their meta-evaluative findings. The first forum will involve members of the evaluation team, key leaders from the school and district, and designated representatives from the Da Vinci Learning Corporation. The second forum will take place at the school or in the community and will involve all interested stakeholders. In this way, the value-engaged evaluator endeavors to be accountable for the quality and meaningfulness of her work to multiple and diverse stakeholders in the context being evaluated.

References

Abma, T. A. (ed.). "Special Issue: Dialogue in Evaluation." *Evaluation,* 2001, 7.

Abma, T. A., and Stake, R. E. "Stake's Responsive Evaluation: Core Ideas and Evolution." In J. C. Greene and T. A. Abma (eds.), *Responsive Evaluation.* New Directions for Evaluation, no. 92. San Francisco: Jossey-Bass, 2001.

Cronbach, L. J., and Associates. *Toward Reform of Program Evaluation.* San Francisco: Jossey-Bass, 1980.

Greene, J. C. "Evaluators as Stewards of the Public Good." Address presented at the Fourth Conference on the Relevance of Assessment and Culture in Evaluation, Tempe, Ariz., Feb. 2003.

Greene, J. C., Benjamin, L., and Goodyear, L. "The Merits of Mixing Methods in Evaluation." *Evaluation,* 2001, 7(1), 25–44.

Guba, E. G., and Lincoln, Y. S. *Fourth Generation Evaluation.* Thousand Oaks, Calif.: Sage, 1989.

Hood, S. "Responsive Evaluation Amistad Style: Perspectives of One African-American Evaluator." In R. Davis (ed.), *Proceedings of the 1998 Robert E. Stake Symposium on Educational Evaluation.* Urbana-Champaign: University of Illinois, 1999.

House, E. R., and Howe, K. R. *Values in Evaluation and Social Research.* Thousand Oaks, Calif.: Sage, 1999.

MacDonald, B "A Political Classification of Evaluation Studies." In D. Hamilton and others, *Beyond the Numbers Game.* New York: Macmillan, 1977.

Schwandt, T. A. *Evaluation Practice Reconsidered.* New York: Peter Lang, 2004.

Stake, R. E. "Program Evaluation, Particularly Responsive Evaluation." In G. F. Madaus, M. Scriven, and D. L. Stufflebeam (eds.), *Evaluation Models: Viewpoints in Educational and Human Services Evaluation.* Norwood, Mass.: Kluwer-Nijhoff, 1987.

Stake, R. E. *Standards-Based and Responsive Evaluation.* Thousand Oaks, Calif.: Sage, 2004.

JENNIFER C. GREENE is a professor of educational psychology at the University of Illinois, Urbana-Champaign.

*Rigorous information on the implementation and
effectiveness of the Da Vinci Model would be produced
by the evaluation proposed in this chapter.*

In Pursuit of Social Betterment:
A Proposal to Evaluate the Da Vinci
Learning Model

Gary T. Henry

Putting evaluation theories into action is a challenge, in part because theories must be adapted to specifics of setting, time, and information needs, which the evaluators come to learn more about during the initial stages of their inquiry. But having evaluators or evaluation theorists plan an evaluation while facing the same set of circumstances presents a level playing field for them to display and their audience to observe differences in approach, methods, and resolution of competing priorities.

In this chapter, I present a proposal that is roughly based on a contingency-based theory of evaluation developed in *Evaluation: An Integrated Framework for Understanding, Guiding, and Improving Policies and Programs* (Mark, Henry, and Julnes, 2000). In this book, my coauthors and I made it clear that our allegiance was not to a method, not to quantitative or qualitative data, not to an approach, not to a particular way to involve others, not even to committing, a priori, to a group or set of individuals whose needs and interests would be prioritized. We explicitly stated that social betterment was the ultimate goal of evaluation and acknowledged that defining social betterment could be contentious. The book was aimed at professional evaluators who would assess the relevant contingencies while working in concert with sponsors and stakeholders to wring the greatest good from a situation where evaluation was sought.

Our definition of the greatest good, stated in the book and clarified in later work (Henry 2000; Henry and Mark, 2003a; Mark and Henry, 2004), was to focus explicitly on an outcome or outcomes that contribute to social betterment and design the evaluation to inform and, eventually, influence attitudes and actions that could realize the outcome. We make it clear that the success of an evaluation should be judged by its outcomes (Mark and Henry, 2004) and that we need more empirical research to understand the outcomes of evaluation (Henry and Mark, 2003b). It is in this vein that I respond to the vignette presented in Chapter Two by taking the role of a professional evaluator, a partner in DGHK Evaluation Associates, and presenting a proposal to evaluate the Da Vinci Learning Model, which, as you will soon discern, is not an evaluation of the Bunche–Da Vinci Learning Academy.

Introduction to the Proposal

Prior to developing the proposal to evaluate the Da Vinci Learning Model, senior partners with DGHK Associates met with Mary García, principal of the Bunche–Da Vinci Learning Academy, and Douglas Chase, superintendent of schools, and subsequently with representatives of eight foundations that participate in the Columbia Educational Affinity Group along with García and Chase. During these meetings, groundwork for the evaluation was laid. First, García explained that she wanted to know if the Da Vinci Learning Model could work for students and, if so, for whom and under what conditions. She presented detailed data and discussed her experiences with the Da Vinci Learning Model during her three years as principal at Bunche–Da Vinci Academy. She was beginning to question whether the model could work at Bunche or in the State of Columbia, with the school's unique demographics and the state's standardized assessment system that is used to determine if student performance was sufficient to meet the Adequate Yearly Progress requirements set forth in the federal No Child Left Behind Act.

For the second meeting, Chase invited potential evaluation sponsors from across the state, and their interests and issues were added to those of García and Chase. Quickly it became clear that most questions were about the Da Vinci Learning Model, including how it was being implemented at the Bunche–Da Vinci Academy, but that these questions could not be answered without comparative data from other schools, including schools that were implementing the Da Vinci Learning Model and those that were not involved in whole-school reform. By the close of the meeting, a consensus had emerged that the evaluation should:

1. Provide information that would compare student performance in Da Vinci Learning Model schools with other elementary schools that were close matches but were not participating in Da Vinci or another whole school reform.
2. Develop and measure a comprehensive list of measurable outcomes that were important for parents, teachers, and community members as well as for administrative purposes.

3. Examine implementation of the model and resource utilization within the schools.
4. Provide information about the extent to which variations in program implementation produced variations in student outcomes.

Guided by these four tenets, DGHK Evaluation Associates has prepared a proposal to evaluate the Da Vinci Learning Model.

1. Summary of the Evaluation Proposal. The Da Vinci Learning Model is a whole-school reform that emphasizes literacy in its proprietary curriculum, immerses teachers and students in a technology-rich environment, extends the school day and school year, and requires smaller class sizes. The model is being implemented in 112 elementary schools across the State of Columbia. While components of the system have been evaluated and were associated with increased student achievement, the model as a whole has not been evaluated for its ability to have an impact on student learning, social behaviors, or student attitudes toward learning; the satisfaction of parents, teachers, or administrators has not been assessed either. DGHK Evaluation Associates has organized an outstanding team with expertise in school reform, evaluation, database construction and management, and statistical design and analysis to evaluate the implementation and outcomes of the Da Vinci Learning Model. The DGHK team proposes to evaluate the Da Vinci Learning Model by working collaboratively to:

1. Conduct a values inquiry to determine the most highly valued outcomes of schooling held by parents, teachers, administrators, and the communities served by schools using the Da Vinci Learning Model.
2. Develop and document the program theory that links the Da Vinci Learning Model (DVLM) to the highly valued outcomes, as well as noting outcomes that are not linked to the DVLM.
3. Assess implementation and instructional practices of the Da Vinci Model in twelve schools, including the Bunche–Da Vinci Learning Academy, by collecting both quantitative and qualitative data.
4. Use a quasi-experimental, matched-pair design (twenty-five Da Vinci schools and twenty-five comparison schools) to evaluate the outcomes of the Da Vinci schools, including an analysis breaking down the Columbia Assessment Program items that are aligned with the Da Vinci Learning Model curriculum and assessments and those that are not.
5. Test the extent to which differences in the outcomes of the Da Vinci schools are related to differences in implementation of the program.
6. Test the effects of the Da Vinci Learning Model for English language learners, children of color, and children living in poverty.

The details for the evaluation are presented in the next four sections of the proposal. Section 4 contains the most detailed statement of the purpose, methods, and products for the four major stages of the evaluation. Plans for ethical and responsible interactions with human subjects and intellectual property rights are presented in Section 5. We begin with our statement of purpose (Section 2) and research questions (Section 3) to clarify our intentions for how the evidence produced by the evaluation will inform future attitudes and actions as well as the specific evidence that will be produced.

2. Purpose of Evaluation. The evaluation aims to contribute to improving education by achieving two distinct but related purposes:

1. To assess the merit and worth of the Da Vinci Learning Model, particularly in the State of Columbia
2. To improve the program's implementation by identifying aspects of the program that are correlated with better outcomes and determine which mechanisms are triggered by the DVLM *and* those that result in improved outcomes

The sponsor for the evaluation is the Education Affinity Group of Columbia Philanthropies, which, in partnership with the Columbia Department of Education, Columbia Association of Independent Schools, Columbia Professional Educators Association, and Columbia State Superintendents Association, will provide representatives to advise DGHK Evaluation Associates on the evaluation and interpretation of the evaluation findings. Leaders of the Da Vinci Corporation have committed to cooperate with the evaluation by supplying data and assisting in determining standards that would constitute implementation fidelity.

The Da Vinci Learning Model seeks to improve the educational achievement and attainment of children who attend its partner schools through (1) increased achievement and school reform in the elementary school that the children attend, (2) increased access to technology, and (3) increased instructional hours and intensity. The evaluation will inform future decisions of those considering adopting the model and provide empirically substantiated recommendations for improving implementation in schools where the model has been already adopted.

3. Research Questions. Evaluations are guided by research questions, whether or not these questions are made explicit in the design. The evaluation is intended to support decisions in schools where the DVLM is currently being implemented. However, given the widespread interest in the Da Vinci Learning Model across the State of Columbia and, indeed, across the rest of the nation, the evaluation is designed to contribute knowledge and aid policymaking in localities and states beyond those currently implementing the DVLM. Given this scope, DGHK has developed five research questions to be addressed in the evaluation of the Da Vinci Learning Model:

1. What do the primary stakeholders, including parents, community members, teachers, and administrators, view as the most highly valued outcomes for the elementary school experience of the children?
2. What theories relate the model's specific activities to the immediate, intermediate, and long-term outcomes? Are these theories supported by evidence, professional judgments, or intentions? Are all highly valued outcomes plausibly related to the Da Vinci whole-school reform model?
3. Is the Da Vinci Learning Model implemented with fidelity according to the intent of its developers? How does implementation vary from school to school?
4. How do the outcomes of schools that have adopted the Da Vinci Learning Model compare to the outcomes of a matched sample of schools after controlling for prior gains and levels in student achievement and other student and family characteristics? Are different types of students more or less positively affected by the DVLM?
5. To what extent does implementation fidelity affect the outcomes of the Da Vinci Learning Model? What variations in implementation account for differences in the valued outcomes of students, if any?

The five questions that will guide the evaluation are intended to be addressed sequentially, integrating information garnered from prior questions into plans to address later questions. For example, determining the activities that constitute implementation fidelity (question 2) will be essential to develop measures of fidelity (question 3) and assess the effects of fidelity on outcomes (question 5). Moreover, we acknowledge that student achievement, as measured by the Columbia State Assessment Program, will be an important outcome for schooling and therefore will be included in the study. These assessment results are used for the purposes of No Child Left Behind requirements to report and achieve Adequate Yearly Progress. Simply put, they cannot be ignored or omitted from the list of important outcomes. However, it is expected that the evaluation will include other measures, such as student attitudes toward school and learning, disruptive behaviors, violations of school rules, and teacher absenteeism, to name a few that may be important to the groups of stakeholders and the advisory committee. As noted in the following section of the proposal, the evaluation will begin with a values inquiry, the results of which will be available for the comprehensive list of outcomes and the identification of measurement instruments.

4. **Structure of Evaluation.** The evaluation has been organized into four stages: values inquiry, program theory development, implementation assessment, and outcome analysis. The first two stages will allow the evaluation team to better specify the data collection and analysis efforts mounted for the last two stages. Given the need to obtain systematic information about which potential outcomes are most highly valued by the

stakeholders and the need to develop a program theory, the last two stages of the evaluation described in this proposal, of necessity, will not provide as detailed an account of measures and methods as would be the case with a completely prescriptive evaluation. The evaluation advisory committee will provide guidance that will enable the team to refine the plans for the latter stages. This design allows the evaluation team to receive a broad base of input from the communities interested in the success of these elementary schools and to rigorously assess the impact of the model, without ignoring the possibility that implementation flaws may have limited success in achieving highly valued outcomes to date. In Table 4.1, we display the four stages of the evaluation and the purpose of each. The first three stages address the first three evaluation questions, respectively, and the final stage addresses questions 4 and 5. Each of the stages is summarized in a table in the four sections of the proposal that follow.

4A. Values Inquiry. Values inquiry is a useful approach to enable evaluators to understand the goals and expected outcomes of an initiative or program that are considered most important to the program's stakeholders (Mark, Henry, and Julnes, 2000; Renger and Bourdeau, 2004). Specifically, this approach offers the opportunity to engage stakeholders of the schools currently implementing the Da Vinci Learning Model in the evaluation. This approach allows the evaluators to develop a prioritized list of the indicators of success from the vantage point of key stakeholder groups (Henry, 2002). The values inquiry will begin by conducting at least three focus groups each in four elementary schools that are currently implementing the DVLM, as noted in Table 4.2. The four schools will be selected as a subsample of the twenty-five Da Vinci Learning Model sites that will be selected for the Outcomes Analysis (Section 4D). We will select the four schools at random from four strata: high-poverty, low-minority enrollments; high-poverty, high-minority enrollments; low-poverty, high-minority enrollments; and low-poverty, low-minority enrollments. The strata will be formed by splitting the schools based on the median values for the 112 DVLM schools on the two variables.

In each school, parents, teachers, and administrators from the school and district will be invited to participate in an after-school focus group at a convenient time. Incentives for participation will be provided. Focus groups will be conducted in Spanish where needed based on the population within the schools. Other languages can be accommodated if the sample demographics indicate a need. The groups will be asked to offer their thoughts about the things that matter most to them about the school and how they define success for the children attending the school and the school as a whole. To encourage the maximum degree of participation and fairness during the deliberations, Cohen's procedural rules for deliberative democracies (1997) will be followed, and each group will be assessed by its participants in terms of House and Howe's criteria: inclusion, deliberation, and dialogue (House and

Table 4.1. The Four Stages of the Evaluation of the Da Vinci Learning Model

1. Values inquiry	Determine valued outcomes of stakeholders (Q1)
2. Program theory development	Develop linkages between activities and outcomes; specify mechanisms and working hypotheses (Q2)
3. Implementation assessment	Develop indicators of implementation fidelity and assess implementation variations (Q3)
4. Outcome analysis	Compare outcomes of Da Vinci and other schools and test mediation (Q4 and Q5)

Table 4.2. Values Inquiry: Purpose, Methods, and Products

Purpose
- Formulate comprehensive list of valued outcomes of elementary schooling
- Compare and contrast the views of key stakeholder groups about the valued outcomes

Methods
- Focus groups of parents, teachers, and administrators in four schools
- Public hearing in twenty-five Da Vinci Learning Model schools
- Survey probability samples of parents, teachers, administrators, and community members

Products
- Ranking of most valued outcomes
- Comparison of stakeholder groups valued outcomes
- List of measurable indicators of school success for evaluation

Howe, 1999). Cohen's overarching requirement is that the "outcomes are democratically legitimate if and only if they could be the object of a free and reasoned agreement among equals," and he establishes "rationally motivated consensus" as the ideal aim of deliberations (1997, pp. 73–74). House and Howe have operationalized their criteria as ten questions, such as, "How authentic is their interaction?" and "Are any major stakeholders excluded?" (1999, p. 113). These questions will be revised into a form that will allow the focus group participants to readily respond.

In addition, an open forum or public hearing will be organized in each of the twenty-five DVLM schools that are selected and agree to participate in the outcome comparisons (see Section 4D for a description of the method used to select this sample). DGHK will obtain the support of local parents' groups, formal and informal, in organizing these forums and will compensate the organizations for their efforts. These forums will take the comprehensive list of valued outcomes identified in the focus groups and obtain comments on them from parents, teachers, and community members. The lists will be prepared in Spanish and English, and the language-minority parents will be consulted in advance in each school to determine if it is most appropriate to hold separate hearings, have simultaneous translation, or develop another alternative that will maximize inclusion and dialogue. Lists from the focus groups will be modified based on the public hearings. Hearings will be conducted with the objectives of Cohen's procedural rules for deliberative democracy as a guide and be assessed by the participants based on their responses to the ten questions proposed by House and Howe (1999).

Finally, probability samples of community members, parents, administrators, and teachers from each school will be asked to rate up to thirty individual outcomes through telephone and Web-based surveys. This will enable DGHK to obtain the best possible representation of opinion, since not all parents will be able to attend meetings or feel comfortable expressing their opinions in open forums. All survey instruments will have parallel forms in Spanish and English and, if needed, will be translated into up to three more languages to ensure that language minorities have a chance to respond. The survey will be used to develop an overall ranking of valued outcomes, weighting each group's responses equally and a group-by-group comparison of the opinions about valued outcomes (Henry, 2002). Also, DGHK Associates will develop a list of measures that could be used for each outcome and make recommendations to the Advisory Committee about how best to include the high-priority indicators in the design.

4B. *Program Theory Development.* The values inquiry will identify the high-priority outcomes to be included in the evaluation. The subsequent program theory development will allow the DGHK team to assess the extent to which the program addresses each of the highly valued outcomes and describe how the program activities can be linked to valued outcomes into a program theory-logic model (PT/LM). One purpose of a PT/LM is to provide stakeholders with a road map describing the sequence of related events connecting the need for the program activities with the program's desired effect. The basic PT/LM is a diagram of the working hypotheses that are embodied in the reform package. It uses words or pictures (or both) to describe the sequence of activities thought to bring about change and how these activities are linked to the results the program is expected to achieve (Kellogg Foundation, 1998). A second purpose is to enable "program managers and evaluators to see more clearly the underlying rationale or logic of a program" (Chen, Cato, and Rainford, 1998–1999, p. 450). In addition to clearly conveying the underlying rationale, PT/LM should depict, in a commonsense manner, the relationship between the underlying rationale of a program and the elements of evaluation, which include resources, activities, immediate, intermediate, and long-term outcomes of a program, along with measurable indicators for each (Chen, Cato, and Rainford, 1998–1999; Dwyer, 1997; McLaughlin and Jordan, 1999).

For this stage, the evaluation team will work with the developers and staff for the Da Vinci Learning Corporation to construct the program theory or a logic model as noted in Table 4.3. The PT/LM development will enable the team to explicate the mechanisms or change processes that underlie the

Table 4.3. Program Theory Development: Purpose, Methods, and Products

Purpose
- Identify linkages between program activities and outcomes
- Develop working hypotheses about why and how the activities trigger specific valued outcomes
- Assess the extent to which the Da Vinci Learning Model is plausibly linked to most highly valued outcomes

Methods
- Conduct logic modeling exercise with Da Vinci developers and school personnel in four schools
- Use model as a basis for developing list of plausible mechanisms or processes through which the activities are translated into valued outcomes

Products
- Logic model mapping program activities on to immediate, intermediate, and long-term outcomes
- List of valued outcomes not plausibly linked to Da Vinci Learning Model
- List of activities and mechanisms to be incorporated into implementation assessment

change process for the reform, providing a road map for the aspects of implementation that form the key to implementation fidelity, and establish explicit working hypotheses on which the success of the DVLM ultimately hinges. The ad hoc theories developed with the model developers and staff will then be traced through the research literature to better understand the extent to which they have been empirically supported and the strength of the data and methods used in prior studies.

To gain from the perspectives of those implementing the DVLM, teachers in four schools (the four focus group sites selected in Section 4A) will be engaged in a logic modeling process (Renger and Titcomb, 2002) to thoroughly explicate the ways that program activities are linked to outcomes. In addition, they will be asked to provide their views about the direct and indirect effects that program activities might have on highly valued outcomes that are not included in their logic models. The activities and the short-term and intermediate-term outcomes will be used by DGHK to develop the list of program implementation measures that will be incorporated into the implementation assessment and analyzed in the outcomes analysis, specifically in response to question 5.

4C. Implementation Assessment. Two approaches to implementation assessment are included in this evaluation. The first is to assess the DVLM schools using a set of indicators for normative standards that collectively constitute implementation fidelity. Second, we will develop a list of implementation variables, including both resource measures and activity measures such as teacher experience and qualifications, instructional practices, and staff professional development activities, that may influence the outcomes of the students. By comparing these measurable indicators of implementation, we can provide a very detailed description of the DVLM resources and activities and compare those to schools that are not using a whole-school reform model. Using both approaches, we will be able to assess the extent to which implementation fidelity is associated with differences in student outcomes and the relationship between local implementation decisions and student outcomes as a part of the outcome analysis (Stage 4). It is extremely important to be able to assess the extent to which implementation may have affected the success of the program, especially if the outcomes do not reach expectations for the DVLM. To draw any conclusions about the utility of the DVLM model, evidence must be presented on the extent to which the outcomes are attributable, at least in part, to implementation flaws or implementation choices that could be altered. Also, findings substantiating variation in outcomes associated with implementation differences may lead to empirically based recommendations for program improvements that are likely to yield better student outcomes.

In large measure, the implementation assessment indicators will be developed from the program theory development activities. Multiple data sources will be used to collect the data needed, and multiple methods will be used to assess program implementation in the DVLM elementary schools (see Table 4.4). These methods include surveying teachers and administrators, classroom observations, and collecting structured reports from teachers concerning their instructional methods, content coverage in math, literacy, and use of technology. Some of the data sources will allow comparison between DVLM schools, and others will allow the DVLM schools to be compared with the matched sample schools.

Teachers and administrators in all fifty schools selected for the outcomes analysis (see Section 4D) will be surveyed about their instructionally related activities as well as their attitudes about teaching and learning processes within their schools. Survey questions will draw from existing, comparable studies and issues gleaned from the values inquiry and program theory development stages. For example, we will ask teachers to provide data about their instructional practices. Their recall about these activities will be aided by the use of structured diaries that encourage them to record the content coverage and instructional methods used daily. Teachers will be provided with incentives for completing the diaries and surveys. We will use the state administrative data to obtain variables that have to do with teachers' education, experience, tenure, and mobility, as well as class sizes and student demographics and assignments.

Classroom observations will allow DGHK evaluators to see how instructional practices targeted in the DVLM are being carried out. Classroom observations will include time sampling to record teachers' instructional approach and content coverage, as well as collecting portfolios containing children's work. Since time on task and intensity of instruction are key features of the

Table 4.4. Implementation Assessment: Purpose, Methods, and Products

Purpose
- Identify key indicators of implementation fidelity
- Measure variation in implementation and degree of implementation fidelity

Methods
- Surveys of teachers and administrators in all fifty schools
- Teacher diaries of instructional practices and content coverage in all fifty schools
- Structured observations of instructional practices in twelve Da Vinci Learning Model schools
- Semistructured interviews with teachers, administrators, and parents in twelve Da Vinci schools

Products
- Assessment of the degree of implementation fidelity in twelve Da Vinci schools
- Comparison of instructional practices, use of technology, and content coverage in twenty-five Da Vinci schools and twenty-five matched schools

Da Vinci approach, these attributes will be carefully recorded. In addition, actual class size at selected intervals will be recorded to measure the implementation of these reform objectives. Finally, particular attention will be paid to the integration of technology into instruction. At each time interval, the use of computers, handheld devices, and audiovisual technology will be recorded. The observation instruments will be adapted from instruments used in an evaluation of teacher professional development (Garet and others, 2001; Desimone and others, 2002) and an evaluation of the effects of the elimination of social promotion on instruction (Roderick and others, 2003).

A subsample of twelve schools from the twenty-five DVLM schools selected for the implementation analysis will be selected for these more intensive classroom observations. The sampling will stratify the twenty-five schools by the percentage of language minorities and the percentage of children living in poverty prior to sampling to ensure the heterogeneity of the schools included. In addition, we plan to conduct semistructured interviews with parents, teachers, and administrators in the twelve schools selected for classroom observations. These interviews can yield more insights about implementation issues and satisfaction or dissatisfaction with specific aspects of the DVLM reform. These interviews will be conducted by trained DGHK staff with experience in schools and familiarity with conducting open-ended interviews. The interviews will involve general prompts about key elements of the reform model, and interviewers will be encouraged to probe to gain a more complete understanding of the responses.

4D. Outcome Analysis. A major motivation for adopting the Da Vinci Learning Model is to improve the achievement and educational attainment of students. And it is important to understand the extent to which the Da Vinci Learning

Table 4.5. Outcome Analysis: Purpose, Methods, and Products

Purpose
- Estimate net effects of Da Vinci Learning Model on valued outcomes
- Estimate net effects of Da Vinci Learning Model on valued outcomes on students performing below grade level and English language learners
- Compare effects of Da Vinci Learning Model on CAP test items aligned with Da Vinci model and those not aligned

Methods
- Collect outcome measures for cohort of students from grade 3 to grade 5 (grade 2 baseline measures)
- Collect outcome measures for children K–3, including direct assessments of language, communication, academic, social behaviors, overall readiness, and well-being
- Compare differences in outcomes of Da Vinci Learning Model schools and matched schools using hierarchical linear and structural equation models testing for mediation and effects of implementation variation

Products
- Analysis of the effects of the Da Vinci program on students in grades 3–5 and K–3
- Analysis of moderated effects for children of color, children living in poverty, English language learners, and children beginning school performing below their peers
- Analysis of mediation and impacts of implementation variation

Model improved performance on the Columbia Assessment Program as a part of this evaluation. However, the outcome analysis will not be limited to test scores and retention rates. The values inquiry will produce a set of highly valued outcomes that will, to the extent possible, be incorporated into the outcome analysis. It will be infeasible to assess the impact of the DVLM on high school graduation or college-going rates during this evaluation, but it may be feasible to measure concurrent indicators of success such as students' attitudes toward school and learning and teacher turnover. The program theory development will produce a schema of working hypotheses that include interrelationships among immediate, intermediate, and longer-term outcomes. From this, a specific plan for measures to be collected and an analysis plan that relies on structural equation modeling can be developed, consistent with a confirmatory evaluation approach (Reynolds, 2000). Moderated effects for different groups of children can be tested in these models as well. In addition, the implementation assessment will identify resources and activities that are to be examined for their empirical linkage to specific outcomes. Finally, the association between implementation fidelity and outcomes will be tested. A summary of the outcomes of this analysis can be found in Table 4.5.

Obviously the specific analyses conducted during this stage of the evaluation will be informed by the three preceding stages, but we are committed, in advance, to the investigation of the robustness of any observed effects of the DVLM. In particular, we will assess whether the effects of the DVLM are similar or different for language minorities, including Latinos, Asian-language students, African American students, and other racial/ethnic minorities for whom sufficient data can be collected to make it feasible to test moderated effects. In addition, moderated effects for children from high-poverty families and children who are behind grade-level expectations on entry to a DVLM school will be assessed.

Multiple measures will be used to assess student achievement based on the program theory that is developed and the values outcomes identified in stages 1 and 2. Baseline measures provide an important component of assessing student achievement for each of the two cohorts whose achievement will be analyzed for this evaluation. We will use end-of-second-grade Columbia Assessment Program (CAP) scores as baselines for the third-grade cohort that will be analyzed and a kindergarten-entry battery of direct assessments of language and cognitive abilities as the baseline measures for the kindergarten cohort. These baselines will allow DGHK Associates to assess the trajectories of the two cohorts and test the differences in growth (slopes) over the three years of the study, as well as the students' performance differences at the end of the three years (intercept centered at the last assessment) by using hierarchical linear modeling (HLM: Bryk and Raudenbush, 1992). Assessment of items aligned with the DVLM on the CAP and those not aligned with the DVLM will be done separately and compared to assess the impact of alignment on the outcomes aligned with DVLM. However, because not all measures will have baseline scores or consistent measurement over the three years of the evaluation—for example, science is not assessed in the CAP until fourth grade, and attitudes toward school are not measured annually—only a few achievement measures can be evaluated using HLM techniques. As mentioned above, structural equation modeling is a preferred alternative for testing mediation, and when it is used, standard errors will be corrected for school-level cluster effects.

Sample selection will be conducted using a probability sample technique. Because of the matched, quasi-experimental design, the sample of Da Vinci Learning Model schools will be drawn first. Using a stratified sampling approach, the evaluation team will choose 25 of the 112 Da Vinci elementary schools in the State of Columbia for the study. The Bunche–Da Vinci Learning Academy will be selected with certainty and properly weighted in the analysis (Henry, 1990). Schools will be stratified by racial/ethnic composition, percentage English language learners, and percentage eligible for free or reduced-price lunch and selected using proportional sampling techniques. Based on currently available data, it appears that the resulting samples are likely to contain a sufficient sample of language minorities and students from high-poverty families.

Comparison schools will be selected using propensity score matching techniques (Rosenbaum, 2002; Rosenbaum and Rubin, 1983; Rubin, 1977). All non-whole-school reform elementary schools in Columbia will be eligible for the matching. Matching variables include test scores for the prior four years, racial/ethnic composition, percentage English language learners, and percentage eligible for free or reduced price lunch. Comparison schools will be selected minimizing the bias estimates using a propensity scoring algorithm. Comparison schools will be provided with Professional Development Funds ($10,000 per school per year) as an incentive to participate in the data collection. The propensity estimates will be used in subsequent analyses to control for selection bias.

Student selection will involve choosing fifty students within each cohort (third grade and kindergarten) in all fifty study schools. These children will be chosen at random from the students entering those grades for the first time in the next academic year. For the third graders, they must have CAP second-grade assessment scores available. Using a power analysis, a sample of this size will provide sufficient power to detect a .25 effect size with 80 percent certainty assuming school level; baseline covariates that are correlated at approximately .80 are available. Larger samples will be used for the analysis of the assessment performance of the third-grade cohort, since the data are available at no additional cost.

In an effort to evaluate programmatic effects on student achievement, two separate data collections will be undertaken. First, direct assessments will be conducted with kindergarten students in both schools at the beginning of the next school year, the end of that school year, and the following two school years. These objective assessments using nationally standardized tests (Peabody Picture Vocabulary Test, Woodcock-Johnson Test of Achievement, and others) allow not only comparisons between the treatment and control schools but also comparisons against national norms (Dunn and Dunn, 1997; Woodcock, McGrew, and Mather, 2001). Finally, assessment scores for the kindergarten sample cohort and all of the third graders in the sample school will be collected for the current and subsequent three school years. Other outcome variables will be collected according to a plan developed by DGHK Associates subsequent to completion of stages 1 and 2 of the evaluation and approved by the Advisory Committee.

5. Human Subjects and Intellectual Property Rights Issues. DGHK Associates will adhere to Institutional Review Board requirements protecting human subjects. All data will be treated confidentially, and protocols will be used to store the data in ways that inhibit individuals not associated with the research team from obtaining any information that can identify the students or their families. The Columbia Department of Education and the participating schools will make available the data as requested and provide access for DGHK Associates to collect the data described in this proposal. For the direct assessments of the kindergarten cohort, informed consent will be obtained from parents prior to including any student in the study. DGHK has a working arrangement with the Institutional Review Board from the State University of Columbia to obtain a review and approval of all human participant procedures prior to initiating this evaluation. The evaluation team will seek a waiver for data not specifically mentioned above based on the exclusion for evaluation of state programs.

The study sponsors, Da Vinci Learning Corporation, and the Advisory Committee for the evaluation will have a minimum of thirty days to review the reports prepared to fulfill the requirements of this evaluation. The DGHK team agrees to consider all comments and make changes in factual information where warranted and to ensure that the findings and any recommendations or conclusions are based on sound and accurate analysis. The evaluation team will have the rights to use the data collected for the purposes of this evaluation in professional, academic, or scholarly publications. The study sponsors, Da Vinci Learning Corporation, and the Advisory Committee for the evaluation will have a minimum of thirty days to review any paper or article prior to submission to such a publication. The authors of such papers from DGHK will consider all comments and make factual changes where warranted. All publications will contain an acknowledgment identifying the source of funding and accepting responsibility for the content of the article and interpretations of the research findings by the author(s) of the manuscript.

6. Conclusions. The proposed evaluation will provide a fair, rigorous, and comprehensive evaluation of the Da Vinci Learning Model as it is currently implemented in the State of Columbia. It is of utmost importance to be fair to key stakeholders and the Da Vinci Corporation. While engaging key stakeholders in meaningful ways throughout the evaluation, the proposal acknowledges and respects the time of key stakeholder groups and maximizes the likelihood that authentic perspectives from all of the groups will be obtained and incorporated into the study. Moreover, the evaluation balances the participation of these stakeholders by including staff and leaders from the Da Vinci Corporation in the development of the program theory and identification of key indicators for implementation fidelity. By testing for implementation flaws, the evaluation team provides a means of distinguishing a failure of program design from lack of fidelity with implementation standards.

The evaluation plan will provide technically accurate evidence in the four-stage design. Sufficient power, state-of-the-art measurement, and sophisticated and appropriate analysis will support the development of accurate comparisons of DVLM and the matched schools. Every effort will be made to conduct the evaluation such that the findings will be able to withstand intense methodological scrutiny and peer review and provide evidence capable of influencing attitudes and actions of stakeholders. Finally, DGHK Associates is committed to maintaining transparency of process and in dissemination of findings through the maintenance of a Web site where pertinent information about the evaluation, including reports, updates, and Advisory Committee meeting notes, will be made accessible.

References

Bryk, A., and Raudenbush, S. W. *Hierarchical Linear Models for Social and Behavioral Research: Applications and Data Analysis Methods.* Thousand Oaks, Calif.: Sage, 1992.

Chen, W. W., Cato, B. M., and Rainford, N. "Using a Logic Model to Plan and Evaluate a Community Intervention Program: A Case Study." *International Quarterly of Community Health Education,* 1998–1999, *18*(4), 449–458.

Cohen, J. "Deliberation and Democratic Legitimacy." In J. Bohman and W. Rehg (eds.), *Deliberative Democracy: Essays on Reason and Politics.* Cambridge, Mass.: MIT Press, 1997.

Desimone, L., and others. "Effects of Professional Development on Teachers' Instruction: Results from a Three-Year Longitudinal Study." *Educational Evaluation and Policy Analysis,* 2002, *24*(2), 81–112.

Dunn, L. M., and Dunn, L. M. *Peabody Picture Vocabulary Test-Third Edition.* Circle Pines, Minn.: American Guidance Service, 1997.

Dwyer, J. "Using a Program Logic Model That Focuses on Performance Measurement to Develop a Program." *Canadian Journal of Public Health,* 1997, *88*(6), 421–425.

Garet, M. S., and others. "What Makes Professional Development Effective? Results from a National Sample of Teachers." *American Educational Research Journal,* 2001, *38*(4), 915–945.

Henry, G. T. *Practical Sampling.* Thousand Oaks, Calif.: Sage, 1990.

Henry, G. T. "Why Not Use?" In V. Caracelli and H. Preskill (eds.), *Evaluation Use.* New Directions for Evaluation, no. 88. San Francisco: Jossey-Bass, 2000.

Henry, G. T. "Choosing Criteria to Judge Program Success: A Values Inquiry." *Evaluation,* 2002, *8*(2), 182–204.

Henry, G. T., and Mark, M. M. "Beyond Use: Understanding Evaluation's Influence on Attitudes and Actions." *American Journal of Evaluation,* 2003a, *24*(3), 293–314.

Henry, G. T., and Mark, M. M. "Toward an Agenda for Research on Evaluation." In C. A. Christie (ed.), *The Practice-Theory Relationship in Evaluation.* New Directions for Evaluation, no. 97. San Francisco: Jossey-Bass, 2003b.

House, E. R., and Howe, K. R. *Values in Evaluation and Social Research.* Thousand Oaks, Calif.: Sage, 1999.

Kellogg Foundation. "Logic Model Development Guide." Battle Creek, Mich., 1998. http://www.wkkf.org/Pubs/Tools/Evaluation/Pub3669.pdf.

Mark, M. M., and Henry, G. T. "The Mechanisms and Outcomes of Evaluation Influence." *Evaluation,* 2004, *10*(1), 35–37.

Mark, M. M., Henry, G. T., and Julnes, G. *Evaluation: An Integrated Framework for Understanding, Guiding, and Improving Policies and Programs.* San Francisco: Jossey-Bass, 2000.

McLaughlin, J. A., and Jordan, G. B. "Logic Models: A Tool for Telling Your Program's Performance Story." *Evaluation and Program Planning,* 1999, *22,* 65–72.

Renger, R., and Bourdeau, B. "Strategies for Values Inquiry: An Exploratory Case Study." *American Journal of Evaluation,* 2004, *25*(1), 39–49.

Renger, R., and Titcomb, A. "A Three-Step Approach to Teaching Logic Models." *American Journal of Evaluation,* 2002, *23*(4), 493–503.

Reynolds, A. J. *Success in Early Interventions: The Chicago Child-Parent Centers.* Lincoln: University of Nebraska Press, 2000.

Roderick, M., and others. *Ending Social Promotion: Results from Summer Bridge.* Chicago: Consortium on Chicago School Research, 2003.

Rosenbaum, P. R. "Attributing Effects to Treatment in Matched Observational Studies." *Journal of the American Statistical Association,* 2002, *97*(457), 183–192.

Rosenbaum, P. R., and Rubin, D. B. "Assessing Sensitivity to an Unobserved Binary Covariate in an Observational Study with Binary Outcome." *Journal of the Royal Statistical Society,* 1983, *45*(2), 212–218.

Rubin, D. B. "Assignment of Treatment Group on the Basis of a Covariate." *Journal of Educational Statistics,* 1977, *2,* 1–26.

Woodcock, R. W., McGrew, K. S., and Mather, N. *Woodcock-Johnson III Tests of Achievement.* Itasca, Ill.: Riverside Publishing, 2001.

GARY T. HENRY is a professor in the Andrew Young School of Policy Studies and Department of Political Science at Georgia State University.

The evaluator in this chapter provides a realistic account
of the actions he would take to provide external
evaluation services using the program theory–
driven evaluation science approach.

Using Program Theory–Driven Evaluation Science to Crack the Da Vinci Code

Stewart I. Donaldson

Program theory–driven evaluation science uses substantive knowledge, as opposed to method proclivities, to guide program evaluations (Donaldson and Lipsey, forthcoming). It aspires to update, clarify, simplify, and make more accessible the evolving theory of evaluation practice commonly referred to as theory-driven or theory-based evaluation (Chen, 1990, 2004, 2005; Donaldson, 2003, forthcoming; Rossi, 2004; Rossi, Lipsey, and Freeman, 2004; Weiss, 1998, 2004a, 2004b).

This chapter describes in some detail how I would respond to the call from Mary García, principal of the Bunche–Da Vinci Learning Partnership Academy, asking my organization, DGHK Evaluation Associates, for a proposal to provide "an evaluation and recommendations for school improvement." Based on specific instructions from the editors, I have attempted to provide a realistic account of the actions I would take to provide evaluation services using the program theory–driven evaluation science approach. While I have avoided the temptation of simply explicating the principles and procedures for conducting program theory–driven evaluation science again (Donaldson, 2003, forthcoming; Donaldson and Gooler, 2003; Donaldson and Lipsey, forthcoming; Fitzpatrick, 2002), I do provide a limited amount of background rationale in key sections to help readers better understand my proposed actions.

This exercise was a stimulating and useful way to think about how I actually work and make decisions in practice. It was obviously not as interactive and dynamic an experience as working with real evaluation clients and

New Directions for Evaluation, no. 106, Summer 2005 © Wiley Periodicals, Inc.

stakeholders. For example, conversations with stakeholders, observations, and other forms of data often uncover assumptions, contingencies, and constraints that are used to make decisions about evaluation designs and procedures. It was necessary at times to make assumptions based on the best information I could glean from the case description and my imagination or best guesses about the players and context. The major assumptions I made to allow me to illustrate likely scenarios are highlighted throughout my evaluation plan. My goal was to be as authentic and realistic as possible about proposing a plan to evaluate this complex program within the confines of everyday, real-world evaluation practice.

Cracking the Da Vinci Code

It is important to recognize that not all evaluation assignments are created equal. Program theory–driven evaluation science, and even external evaluation more generally, may not be appropriate or the best approach for dealing with some requests for evaluation. The Bunche–Da Vinci case, as presented, suggested that one or more of a highly complex set of potentially interactive factors might account for the problems it faced or possible ultimate outcome of concern: declining student performance. Principal Mary García appears exasperated, and district superintendent Douglas Chase at a loss for how to deal with the long list of seemingly insurmountable challenges for the Bunche–Da Vinci Learning Partnership Academy. Why has such a good idea gone bad? Why is performance declining? Could it be due to:

- A changing population?
- Social groupings of students?
- Student attendance problems?
- The curriculum?
- The innovative technology?
- Language barriers?
- Culturally insensitive curriculum and instruction?
- Staff turnover?
- The teachers' performance?
- Parenting practices?
- Leadership problems?
- Organizational problems?

And the list of questions could go on and on. How do we crack this "code of silence" or solve this complex mystery? "We've got it," say García and Chase. "Let's just turn to the Yellow Pages and call our local complex problem solvers: DGHK Evaluation Associates."

It appears to me on the surface that DGHK Evaluation Associates is being called in to help "solve" some seemingly complex and multidimensional instructional, social, personnel, and possibly leadership and organizational problems. What I can surmise from this case description, among other characteristics, is:

- There appear to be many factors and levels of analysis to consider.
- Everyone is a suspect at this point (including García and Chase).

Some of the stakeholders in this case may have different understandings, views, and expectations about evaluation, and some may be very apprehensive or concerned about the powerful school administrators calling in outsiders to evaluate program and stakeholder performance.

The conditions listed above can be a recipe for external evaluation disaster, particularly if this case is not managed carefully and effectively. As a professional external evaluator, I do not have the magic tricks in my bag that would make me feel confident about guaranteeing Bunche–Da Vinci that I could solve this mystery swiftly and convincingly. However, I would be willing to propose a process and plan that I believe would stand a reasonable chance of yielding information and insights that could help them improve the way they educate their students. So how would I use and adapt program theory–driven evaluation science to work on this caper?

Negotiating a Realistic and Fair Contract

In my opinion, one of the key lessons from the history of evaluation practice is that program evaluations rarely satisfy all stakeholders' desires and aspirations. Unrealistic or poorly managed stakeholder expectations about the nature, benefits, costs, and risks of evaluation can quickly lead to undesirable conflicts and disputes, lack of evaluation use, and great dissatisfaction with evaluation teams and evaluations (see Donaldson, 2001a; Donaldson, Gooler, and Scriven, 2002). Therefore, my number one concern at this initial entry point was to develop realistic expectations and a contract that was reasonable and fair to both the stakeholders and the evaluation team.

The Bunche–Da Vinci Learning Partnership is a well-established, ongoing partnership program, with a relatively long (more than three years) and complex history. Therefore, I made the following two assumptions prior to my first meeting with García and Chase:

Assumption: There are serious evaluation design and data collection constraints. This is a very different situation from the ideal evaluation textbook case where the evaluation team is involved from the inception of the program and is commissioned to conduct a needs assessment, help with program design and implementation, and design the most rigorous outcome and efficiency evaluations possible.

Assumption: Money is an object. Based on the case description, I assumed that García and Chase desired the most cost-effective evaluation possible. That is, even if they do have access to substantial resources, they would prefer to save as much of those as possible for other needs, such as providing more educational services.

It is important to note here that I would approach aspects of this evaluation very differently if money were no object (or if the evaluation budget were specified), and there were fewer design or data collection constraints.

Meeting 1. My first meeting with García and Chase was a success. I began the meeting by asking each of them to elaborate on their views about the nature of the program and its success and challenges. Although they had different views and perceptions at times, they seemed to genuinely appreciate that I was interested in their program and daily concerns. They also said they were relieved that I began our relationship by listening and learning, and not by lecturing them about my credentials, evaluation methods, measurement, and statistics, like some of the other evaluators with whom they have worked.

After García and Chase felt that they had provided me with what they wanted me to know about the partnership, I asked them to share what they hoped to gain by hiring an external evaluation team. In short, they wanted us to tell them why their state scores had declined and how to reverse this personally embarrassing and socially devastating trend. It was at that point that I began to describe how DGHK Evaluation Associates could provide evaluation services that might shed light on ways to improve how they were currently educating their students.

In an effort to be clear and concise, I started by describing in common language a simple three-step process that the DGHK Evaluation Team would follow:

1. We would engage relevant stakeholders in discussions to develop a common understanding of how the partnership is expected to enhance student learning and achievement. This is Step 1: Developing Program Theory. (Note that I rarely use the term *program theory* with stakeholders because it is often confusing and sometimes perceived as high brow and anxiety provoking.)
2. Once we have a common understanding or understandings (multiple program theories), I explain that we would engage relevant stakeholders in discussion about potential evaluation questions. This is Step 2: Formulating and Prioritizing Evaluation Questions.
3. Once stakeholders have identified the most important questions to answer, we will then help them design and conduct the most rigorous empirical evaluation possible within practical and resource constraints. Relevant stakeholders will also be engaged at this step to discuss and determine the types of evidence needed to accurately answer the key questions. This is Step 3: Answering Evaluation Questions.

In general, I pledged that our team would strive to be as accurate and useful as possible, as well as participatory, inclusive, and empowering as the context will allow. That is, sometimes stakeholders may choose not to be included, participate, or use the evaluation to foster program improvement and self-determination. At other times, resource and practical constraints limit the degree to which these goals can be reached in an evaluation. García and Chase seemed to like the general approach, but after they thought about it some more, they began to ask questions. They seemed particularly surprised by (and possibly concerned about) the openness of the approach and the willingness of the evaluation team to allow diverse stakeholder voices to influence decisions about the evaluation. They asked me if this was my unique approach to evaluation or if it was commonly accepted practice these days. I acknowledged that there are a variety of views and evaluation approaches (Alkin and Christie, 2004; Donaldson and Scriven, 2003), but pointed out that the most widely used textbooks in the field are now based on or give significant attention to this approach (examples are Rossi, Lipsey, and Freeman, 2004; Weiss, 1998). Furthermore, I revealed that many federal, state, and local organizations and agencies now use similar evaluation processes and procedures. They seemed relieved that I had not just cooked up my approach in isolation as a fancy way to share my opinions and render judgments. However, they did proceed to push me to give a specific example of one of these organizations or agencies. So I briefly described the Centers for Disease Control's six-step Program Evaluation Framework (1999).

The CDC Evaluation Framework is not only conceptually well developed and instructive for evaluation practitioners, it has been widely adopted for evaluating federally funded programs throughout the United States. This framework was developed by a large group of evaluators and consultants in an effort to incorporate, integrate, and make accessible to public health practitioners useful concepts and evaluation procedures from a range of evaluation approaches. Using the computer in García's office, I quickly downloaded Figure 5.1 from the CDC Web site.

I then proceeded to describe the similarities of the three- and six-step approaches. I explained that the first two steps of the CDC framework (engage stakeholders and describe the program) corresponded to what I described as the first step of the Bunche–Da Vinci Evaluation. The activities of CDC step 3 (focus the evaluation design) are what we will accomplish in the second step I described, and CDC steps 4 to 6 (gather credible evidence, justify conclusions, and ensure use and lessons learned) correspond to what we will achieve in step 3 of the Bunche–Da Vinci Evaluation. In addition, I explained how the standards for effective evaluation (utility, feasibility, propriety, and accuracy; Joint Committee on Standards for Educational Evaluation, 1994) and the American Evaluation Association's Guiding Principles (systematic inquiry, competence, integrity/honesty, respect for people, and responsibilities for general and public welfare; AEA Guiding Principles for Evaluators, 2004) are realized using this evaluation approach. Well, that did it; García and Chase were exhausted. They asked me if I could meet with them again next week to further discuss establishing an evaluation contract.

Figure 5.1. CDC Six-Step Evaluation Framework

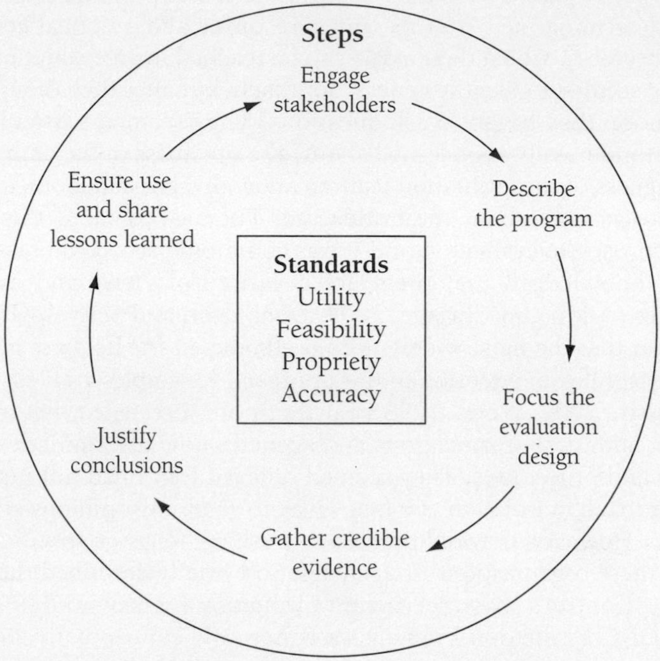

Source: Centers for Disease Control (1999).

Meeting 2. I could tell a considerable amount of discussion had occurred since our initial meeting. While it was clear they were eager to proceed, I could sense I was about to be bombarded with more questions. First, García wanted to know who would be engaging the stakeholders and facilitating the meetings to discuss the program and evaluation. My guess is she was concerned that I (a highly educated European American male) would be perceived as a threatening outsider and might not be the best choice for engaging her predominantly Latino and African American students, parents, staff, and teachers. This gave me the opportunity to impress on her that personnel recruitment, selection, and management is one of the most critical components of conducting a successful evaluation. She seemed to get this point when she thought about it in terms of problems she has encountered running her school. I assured her that we would strive to assemble a highly competent and experienced team with a particular emphasis on making sure we have team members knowledgeable about the program, context, and the evaluation topics we pursue. We would also make sure that we hire team members who share key background characteristics such as ethnicity, culture, language, and sociocultural experiences, and who possessed the ability to understand and build trusting and productive relationships with the various stakeholder groups represented at the Bunche–Da Vinci Learning Academy. Furthermore, we would request funds to support hiring top-level experts to consult with us on topics we encounter that require highly specialized expertise. She very much liked the idea of supporting the assembly of a multicultural team as part of the evaluation contract.

Next, Chase wanted to know if there were any risks or common problems associated with engaging stakeholders. After reminding him of the potential benefits, I described some of the risks related to external evaluation in general, as well as to the evaluation plan I was proposing. For example, it is possible that various stakeholders (for example, the Da Vinci Learning Corporation administration or staff) will refuse to participate, provide misleading information, or undermine the evaluation in other ways. The evaluation findings might deliver various types of bad news, including uncovering unprofessional or illegal activities, and result in serious consequences for some stakeholders. Precious time and resources that could be used to provide services to needy students could be wasted if the evaluation is not accurate, useful, and cost-effective (see Donaldson, 2001a; Donaldson, Gooler, and Scriven, 2002, for more possible risks). Of course, I explained there are also serious risks associated with not evaluating at this point and that we would attempt to identify, manage, and prevent risks or negative consequences of our work every step of the way. He seemed pleasantly surprised that I was willing to discuss the dark side of external evaluation and was not just another evaluation salesperson.

After fielding a number of other good questions, concerns about budget and how much all this professional evaluation service will cost emerged in our discussion. I proposed to develop separate budgets for the conceptual work to be completed in steps 1 and 2 and the empirical evaluation work to be completed in step 3. That is, we would be willing to sign a contract that enabled us to complete the first two steps of developing program theory and formulating and prioritizing evaluation questions. Based on the mutual satisfaction and agreement of both parties, we would sign a second contract to carry out the empirical work necessary to answer the evaluation questions that are determined to be of most importance to the stakeholders.

Our evaluation proposal is intended to be cost-effective and to potentially save both parties a considerable amount of time and resources. During the completion of the first contract, Bunche–Da Vinci stakeholders will be able to assess the effectiveness of the evaluation team in this context and determine how much time and resources they want to commit to empirical data collection and evaluation. This first contract would provide enough resources and stability for our DGHK Evaluation Team to explore fully and better understand the program, context, stakeholders, and design and data collection constraints before committing to a specific evaluation design and data collection plan.

García and Chase seemed enthusiastic about the plan. They were ready to draw up the first contract so we could get to work. However, it dawned on them that some of their key colleagues were still out of the loop. They began to discuss which one of them would announce and describe the evaluation to their colleagues. At that point, I offered to help. I suggested that they identify the leaders of the key stakeholder groups. After introducing and conveying their enthusiasm for the idea and the DGHK Evaluation Team (preferably in person or at least by telephone, as opposed to email), they would invite these leaders to an introductory meeting where the evaluation team would provide a brief overview of the evaluation plan and invite them to ask questions. García and Chase invited corporate, faculty, staff, parent, and student representatives to our next meeting to learn more about the evaluation plan.

I have tried to provide a realistic account of how I would attempt to negotiate an evaluation contract with these potential clients. As part of this dialogue, I have simulated the types of discussions and questions I commonly encounter in practice. I would assemble a multicultural team (drawing on existing DGHK Associates staff) to introduce the evaluation plan to the larger group of stakeholder leaders. The presentation would aim to be at about the same level as above, with some additional tailoring to reach and be sensitive to the audience.

Evaluation Plan

In this section, I add some flesh to the bones of the evaluation plan proposed. More specifically, I provide a brief rationale for each step, more details about the actions we will take, and some examples of what might happen as a result of our actions at each step of the plan. To stay within the bounds of this hypothetical case and intellectual exercise, I thought it would be useful to use a format that provides readers a window on how I would describe the Bunche-Da Vinci evaluation to prospective evaluation team members. Therefore, I will strive to illustrate the level of discussion and amount of detail I would typically provide to the candidates being interviewed for the DGHK Associates Multicultural Evaluation Team. My goal is to illustrate how I would provide a realistic job preview to those interested in joining the team, as a way to help readers gain a deeper understanding of my evaluation plan. Realistic job previews are popular human resource selection and organizational socialization interventions that involve explaining both desirable aspects of a job and potential challenges upfront, in an effort to improve person-job fit and performance and reduce employee dissatisfaction and turnover (Donaldson and Bligh, forthcoming).

Bunche–Da Vinci Realistic Job Preview

The evaluation of the Bunche–Da Vinci partnership will use a program theory–driven evaluation science framework. It will emphasize engaging relevant stakeholders from the outset to develop a common understanding of the program in context and realistic expectations about evaluation. We will accomplish this by tailoring the evaluation to meet agreed-on values and goals. That is, a well-developed conceptual framework (program theory) will be developed and then used to tailor empirical evaluation work to answer as many key evaluation questions as possible within project resource and feasibility constraints. A special emphasis will be placed on making sure the evaluation team members, program theory, evaluation questions, evaluation procedures, and measures are sensitive to the cultural differences that are likely to emerge in this evaluation.

Step 1: Developing Program Theory. Our first task will be to talk to as many relevant stakeholders as possible to develop an understanding of how the Bunche–Da Vinci program is expected to meet the needs of its target population. For efficiency, we will work with four or five groups of five to seven stakeholders' representatives to gain a common understanding of the purposes and details about the operations of the program. Specifically, you (interviewee) will be asked to lead or be part of an interactive process that will make implicit stakeholder assumptions and understandings of the program explicit. [See Donaldson and Gooler (2003) and Fitzpatrick (2002) for a detailed discussion and examples of this interactive process applied to actual cases.]

Let me give you an example based on some of the characteristics and concerns I have learned so far. The Bunche–Da Vinci Learning Partnership Academy is an elementary school located in a tough neighborhood. It is a unique partnership between the school district and a nonprofit educational company specializing in innovative school interventions for low-performing students. The school population is characterized by high transience, illegal enrollments from the adjacent district, high numbers of non-English-speaking students, high levels of poverty, a young and inexperienced staff with high turnover, and geographical isolation from the rest of the district. The principal and superintendent are concerned that the partnership program is not an effective way to educate their students. They have shared with me a number of hunches they have about why the program is not working, and the principal has some ideas about how to change and improve the school. But it is important to keep in mind that as we engage other stakeholders in discussions about the program, we are likely to gain a wealth of additional information and possibly hear extremely different views about the program's success and challenges.

After we collect and process the information we gather in the stakeholder meetings, we will attempt to isolate program components, expected short-term outcomes, more long-term or ultimately desired outcomes, and potential moderating factors (Donaldson, 2001b). For example, student performance on state test scores has been the main desired outcome discussed in the conversations I have had with the school administrators. Other stakeholders may strongly object to the notion that the program is designed to improve state test scores and be upset by the No Child Left Behind legislation and accountability zeitgeist. In fact, I expect they will provide us with a range of other desired outcomes to consider as we try to gain a deep understand of the program. However, the program's impact on student performance will likely end up being one of the desired outcomes we explore conceptually and potentially evaluate.

Figure 5.2 shows an example of how we would begin to diagram and probe stakeholders' views about program impact on student performance. The anchor of this program impact theory is student performance. It assumes that the partnership program compared to no program or an alternative (for example, a typical curriculum in a comparable school) is expected to improve student performance. Our discussion with the stakeholders would attempt to clarify why or how the partnership program is presumed to accomplish this. We may discover that there are the key short-term outcomes or mediating factors (represented by the question marks at this point) that are expected to result from the program, which in turn are expected to lead to improved student performance. Once we have clarified these expected mediating processes, we will begin to probe whether these links are expected to be the same for all students and in all context variations that may exist across the delivery of the program. If not, we will isolate the key student characteristics (such as gender, ethnicity, socioeconomic status, language, acculturation, attendance) and potential contextual factors (such as group or class dynamics, instructor effects, service delivery characteristics, and the like) that could moderate or condition the strength or direction of the arrows in our program impact theory. Our ultimate goal is to work through this interactive process with the diverse stakeholder groups until we have a common understanding about the purposes and expected benefits and outcomes of the program.

Once we have completed this process with the stakeholders, you and the other members of the team will be required to assess the plausibility of the stakeholders' program theory or theories. You will do this by reviewing the available research and evaluation literature related to factors identified. We will specifically look for evidence that may suggest that some of the links are not plausible or that there may be side effects or unintended consequences we have not considered. The findings from the review, analysis, and team discussions may lead us to suggest that the stakeholders consider revising or making some additions to their program theory(ies). I expect it will take us at least three months of full-time work to complete this first step of our evaluation plan.

Step 2: Formulating and Prioritizing Evaluation Questions. Once we have a deep understanding of the program and context, we will focus on illuminating empirical evaluation options for the stakeholders. You and the rest of the team will be asked to frame potential evaluation questions so that they are as concrete and specific as possible and informed by the program theory(ies). The types of questions that will likely be considered in the Bunche–Da Vinci evaluation fall under the categories of program need, design, delivery or

Figure 5.2. Example of Program Impact Theory

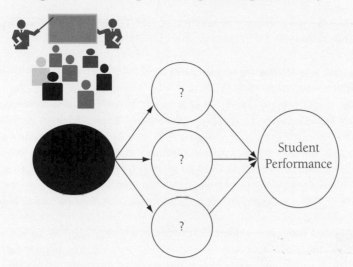

implementation, outcomes, cost, and efficiency (see Rossi, Lipsey, and Freeman, 2004).

My best guess, based on what we know so far about the partnership program, is that we will most likely pursue questions about curriculum implementation, program operations and educational services delivery, and program outcomes. For example, the stakeholders may decide that they want empirical data to answer questions such as:

- Are administrative and educational service objectives being met?
- Are the intended curricula being delivered with high fidelity to the intended students?
- Are there students or families with unmet needs that the program is not reaching?
- Do sufficient numbers of students attend and complete the curriculum?
- Are teachers and students satisfied with the curriculum and educational services?
- Are administrative, organizational, and personnel functions of the partnership program effective?

Furthermore, questions about program outcomes will likely include:

- Are the desired short-term outcomes (mediators) being achieved?
- Are the desired longer-term or ultimate outcomes of concern being achieved?
- Does the program have any adverse side effects?

- Are some recipients affected more by the program than others (moderator effects)?
- Does the program work better under some conditions than others (moderator effects)?

It is possible that we will be asked to pursue questions about the partnership program cost and efficiency—for example, (1) Are the resources being used efficiently? (2) Is the cost reasonable in relation to the benefits? (3) Would alternative educational approaches yield equivalent or more benefits at less cost? Furthermore, García does have some ideas for changing the program and may ask us to answer questions about student needs and best ways to satisfy those needs. But I do think it is likely you will be pursuing questions about program implementation and outcomes if both parties decide to enter into a second contract to collect data to answer the stakeholders' evaluation questions.

Once a wide range of potential evaluation questions has been formulated, you and the DGHK Evaluation Team will help the stakeholders prioritize the questions so that it is clear which questions are of most value. You will need to note differences of opinion about the value of each question across the stakeholder groups and factor them into final decisions about which questions to pursue in the evaluation. In an ideal evaluation world, the entire range of relevant evaluation questions would be answered, and the program impact theory would be tested in the most rigorous fashion possible. However, in most evaluations, only a subset of questions and components of a program impact theory can be evaluated due to time, resource, and practical constraints. Prioritizing and identifying the most important evaluation questions can prevent paralysis in evaluation (that is, deciding to wait or not to evaluate at all). Recognizing that some key questions can be addressed, even though some or many components of the program impact theory and other evaluation questions cannot be examined at this time, will help you to facilitate the evaluation process to move forward.

Finally, it is important for you to realize as a prospective employee and team member that the stakeholders may decide that they have learned enough about the program after we complete these first two steps. For example, it is not uncommon to discover that a program is obviously not being implemented as intended. This could lead the stakeholders to focus their attention and resources on fixing the program, or they may determine it is not repairable and decide to terminate the program and replace it with a promising alternative. If this type of situation develops, it is possible we would obtain an evaluation contract to help them develop and evaluate the new initiative, or we are likely to have another interesting evaluation contract in the firm that you could be hired to work on.

Step 3: Answering Evaluation Questions. Assuming the stakeholders decided they wanted to enter into the second contract with us to answer key evaluation questions, you would be asked to help design and work on an evaluation that would strive to answer those questions convincingly. In many respects, our evaluation approach is method neutral. We believe that quantitative, qualitative, or mixed methods designs are neither superior nor applicable in every evaluation situation (Chen, 1997; Reichhart and Rallis, 1994). Instead, our methodological choices in this evaluation will be informed by program theory, the specific evaluation questions the stakeholders have ranked in order of priority, validity and use concerns, and resource and practical constraints (feasibility). Your main charge at this stage of the evaluation plan is to determine what type of evidence is needed and obtainable, to answer stakeholder questions of interest with an acceptable level of confidence.

As you might know, several factors typically interact to determine how to collect the evidence needed to answer the key evaluation questions such as stakeholder preferences, feasibility issues, resource constraints, and evaluation team expertise. Program theory–driven evaluation science is primarily concerned with making sure the data collection methods are systematic and rigorous, and produce accurate data, rather than privileging one method or data collection strategy over another (see Donaldson and Christie, forthcoming).

It is typically highly desirable to design evaluations so that stakeholders agree up front that the design will produce credible results and answer the key evaluation questions. Participation and buy-in can increase the odds that stakeholders will accept and use evaluation results that do not confirm their expectations or desires. Of course, making sure the design conforms to the Joint Committee Standards (Joint Committee on Standards for Education Evaluation, 1994) and the American Evaluation Association's *Guiding Principles for Evaluators* (2004) as much as possible is also helpful for establishing credibility, confidence, and use of the findings.

The challenge for us in the Bunche–Da Vinci Evaluation will be to gain agreement among the diverse stakeholder groups about which questions to pursue and the types of evidence to gather to answer those key questions. For example, we should be able to gather data from students, teachers, school and corporate administration and staff, parents, and experts in areas of concern. Furthermore, if needed, it looks as if we will be able to collect and access data using existing performance measures and data sets, document and curriculum review, interview methods, Web-based and traditional survey methods, possibly observational methods, focus groups, and expert analysis.

As a member of the evaluation team, your role at this stage of the process will be to help facilitate discussions with the relevant stakeholders about the potential benefits and risks of using the range of data sources and methods available to answer each evaluation question of interest. You will be required to educate the stakeholders about the likelihood that each method under consideration will produce accurate data. You will need to discuss potential threats to validity and possible alternative explanations of findings (Shadish, Cook, and Campbell, 2002), the likelihood of obtaining accurate and useful data from the method in this specific situation, research with human participants (especially with minors), and informed-consent concerns, and to estimate the cost of obtaining data using each method under consideration. Once the stakeholders are fully informed, your job will be to facilitate a discussion that leads to agreement about which sources and methods of data collection to use to answer the stakeholders' questions. This collaborative process will also include reaching agreement on criteria of merit (Scriven, 2003) or agreeing on what would constitute success or failure or a favorable or unfavorable outcome, which will help us justify evaluation conclusions and recommendations. If you are successful at fully informing and engaging the stakeholders, we believe it is much more likely that the stakeholders will accept, use, and disseminate the findings and lessons learned. If you will allow me to make some assumptions, I can give you examples of how this third step of our evaluation plan could play out in the Bunche–Da Vinci evaluation you would be hired to work on.

First, I must underscore that the information we have so far is from the school administrators. That is, once we hear from the teachers, parents, students, and corporate administration and staff, we may gain a different account of the situation. In our view, it would be a fundamental error at this point to base the evaluation on this potentially limited perspective and not include the other stakeholders' views. Nevertheless, I will make some assumptions based on their perspectives to illustrate the process that you will be asked to facilitate at this stage of the evaluation.

Assumption: The stakeholders have decided that their top priority for the evaluation is to determine why the two separate indicators of student performance (state test scores; Da Vinci test scores) provide substantially different results.

García and Chase have suggested that their top concern is that student performance, particularly on the English–Language Arts components of state standards tests, has declined over the course of the partnership program. In fact, in the most recent testing (year 3), students scored lower than in years 1 and 2. These decreasing state test scores contrasted sharply with their corporate partner's assessments of students' performance. On the company's measures, the percentage of students reading at grade level had doubled over the past three years. Da Vinci staff from headquarters claimed to have heard students say that they were "finally able to read" and were much more enthusiastic learners. García and Chase are greatly concerned about this discrepancy.

Assumption: We will assume that the stakeholders have produced Figure 5.2 and that increasing student performance is one of the main purposes of the Partnership Program.

In this case, we would explore all of the strengths and weaknesses of the feasible options for determining why measures of student performance are yielding different results. I would expect the stakeholders to decide to have us conduct a systematic and rigorous analysis of the construct validity of each set of measures. We would pay particularly close attention to potential differences in construct validity across our diverse and changing student body. In addition to the expertise on our team, we would likely hire top-level consultants with specific expertise in student performance measurement in similar urban school environments to help us shed light on the discrepancies. It will be critical at this stage of the evaluation to decide whether the performance problems are real or an artifact of inadequate measurement that can be explained by threats to construct validity (Shadish, Cook, and Campbell, 2002). Imagine the implications of the potential evaluation finding that performance is not really declining or if corporate measures are seriously (possibly intentionally) flawed.

Assumption: The stakeholders decided that their second priority is to determine if the partnership program curriculum is being implemented as planned with high fidelity.

We will have learned much about the design of the curriculum and why it is believed to be better than the alternatives during steps 1 and 2 of our evaluation process. It will be your job as a member of the evaluation team to help verify whether the curriculum is actually being implemented as intended. As is sometimes the case in educational settings, school administrators suspect the teachers might be the main problem. They have suggested to us that teachers have not bought into the partnership program, may even resent its requirements and added demands, and may just be going through the motions. They have also suggested to us that the teachers are young and inexperienced and may not have the motivation, expertise, and support necessary to implement the program with high fidelity. Furthermore, there are some doubts about whether groups of students are fully participating in the program and adequately completing the lesson plans. The rather dramatic changes in the student population may have affected the quality of the implementation of the curriculum.

After considering the available data collection options for answering this question, I would expect you and the evaluation team to be asked to observe and interview representative samples of teachers about the delivery of the Bunche–Da Vinci curriculum. You could also be asked to gather data from students and parents about their experiences with the curriculum. For these technology-enriched students, I would expect that a Web-based survey could be designed and completed by many of the students. However, alternative measurement procedures would need to be developed for those too young to complete a Web-based survey. Furthermore, a representative sample of students could be interviewed in more depth. For the parents, I would expect we would need to design a standard paper-and-pencil survey and be able to interview and possibly conduct some focus groups to ascertain their views and experiences. Finally, interviews of key staff members of both the school district and corporate partner would be pursued to further develop our understanding of how well the curriculum has been implemented and how to improve implementation moving forward. Keep in mind that even if we do find valid student performance indicators in the previous analysis, they could be meaningless in terms of evaluating the partnership program if the program has not been implemented with high fidelity.

The final example of a question that could be pursued in step 3 of the Bunche–Da Vinci Evaluation focuses on determining whether desired short-term outcomes have resulted from the program. For this example, I will assume that the partnership program has been implemented with high fidelity. Figure 5.2 shows that three main short-term outcomes are expected to result from the partnership program. Let us assume that the stakeholders have agreed that the first one is a high level of intrinsic engagement of the curriculum. That is, the program produces a high level of intrinsic engagement, which in turn is expected to lead to increases in student performance.

Assumption: The stakeholders decided their third priority is to assess whether Bunch–Da Vinci students have a high level of intrinsic engagement.

Imagine that after weighing the options, the stakeholders have decided that they would like us to measure and determine whether students at Bunche–Da Vinci have a high level of intrinsic engagement with the curriculum. You and the team would be asked to work with the stakeholders to develop a clear understanding and definition of this construct. Next, we would search and critically review the literature to determine if there are good measures of this construct that could be used for this purpose. Assuming we have identified a strong measurement instrument (we would need to create one otherwise), we would then develop another set of measurement procedures for the students to complete (or include the items on the previous instruments used above, if possible). We would also make sure that we included items about key student characteristics of concern (such as ethnicity, language, acculturation, family, attitudes toward technology, and the like) and characteristics of the context (peer group dynamics and out-of-class study environment, for example), exploring if there may be important moderating influences on the link between the program and this short-term outcome. This will allow us to do more finely grained analyses to estimate whether the program is affecting this short-term outcome more for some students than others.

We will assume that for this initial examination of intrinsic engagement, we do not have a reasonable comparison group or baseline data available. Therefore, prior to implementation, we will gain agreement with the stakeholders about how we will define high versus low levels of intrinsic engagement (that is, establish criteria of merit). Finally, against our recommendation, we will assume that the stakeholders have decided not to survey or interview parents or teachers about intrinsic engagement due to their lack of enthusiasm about spending additional resources for their third priority evaluation question.

As I hope you can now appreciate, working on the DGHK Evaluation of Bunche–Da Vinci promises to be a meaningful opportunity for you. You will be part of a multicultural team of evaluation professionals engaged in helping to address a socially important set of concerns. The course of these children's educational careers and lives could be undermined if we find that this situation is as bad as it appears on the surface and sound recommendations for improvement are not found and implemented in the near future. I would now like to hear more about why your background, skills, and career aspirations make you a strong candidate for being an effective member of the DGHK/Bunche–Da Vinci Evaluation Team. But first, do have any further questions about the job requirements?

Reflections and Conclusions

The Bunche–Da Vinci Case presented DGHK Evaluation Associates with a challenging mystery to be solved. A highly complex set of potentially interactive factors appears to be suspect in the apparent demise of an innovative partnership program. Whomever or whatever is the culprit in this case seems to be responsible for undermining the performance of a diverse and disadvantaged group of students. In the face of this complexity, DGHK Associates has proposed to use a relatively straightforward three-step process to develop and conduct evaluation services to help crack the Da Vinci Code and to potentially improve the lives and trajectories of these children. The proposed evaluation approach is designed to provide cost-effective, external evaluation services. DGHK Associates promises to strive to provide evaluation services that are as accurate and useful as possible to the Bunche–Da Vinci stakeholders, as well as to work in a manner that is participatory, inclusive, and as empowering as stakeholders and constraints will permit.

In an effort to achieve these promises, I have proposed to tailor the evaluation to contingencies our team encounters as they engage stakeholders in the evaluation process. Obviously, to complete this exercise of describing how program theory–driven evaluation science could be adapted and applied to this hypothetical case, I had to make many assumptions. Examples of the details of each step could be substantially different in practice if different assumptions were made. For example, if I assumed the stakeholders wanted us to propose how we would determine the impact of the program on student performance outcomes using a rigorous and resource-intensive randomized control trial (or quasi-experimental design, longitudinal measurement study, intensive case study, or something else), the particulars of the three steps would differ substantially. However, it is important to emphasize that the overall evaluation plan and process I proposed would be virtually the same.

The sample dialogue with the school administrators during the contracting phase and in the realistic job preview I gave to the potential evaluation team members were intended to be helpful for understanding how I provide evaluation services in real-world settings. Based on the case description, I predicted this evaluation would need to operate under somewhat tight resource and practical constraints and would be likely to uncover intense conflicts and dynamics among stakeholder groups. I tried to underscore the point that a fatal flaw would have been to design an evaluation plan in response to information and views provided almost entirely by one powerful stakeholder group (the school administrators, in this case). It seemed likely that the teachers and teachers' union may have made some different attributions (for example, management, leadership, and organizational problems) about the long list of problems and concerns the administrators attributed to the "young and inexperienced" teachers. It also seemed likely that the corporate leadership and staff could have a very different take on the situation. Based on my experience, I am confident that the failure to incorporate these types of stakeholder dynamics in the evaluation plan and process would likely undermine the possibility of DGHK Associates' producing an accurate and useful evaluation for the Bunche–Da Vinci Learning Partnership.

It would have also been problematic to conduct extensive (and expensive) data collection under the assumption that student performance had actually declined. That is, a considerable amount of evaluation time and resources could have been expended on answering questions related to why performance had declined over time, when in fact performance was not declining or even improving, as one of the indicators suggested. Therefore, in this case, it seemed crucial to resolve the discrepancy between the performance indicators before pursuing evaluation questions based on the assumption that performance had actually declined.

Due to space limitations, there are aspects of this case and evaluation plan I was not able to explore or elaborate on in much detail. For example, during the developing program theory phase of the evaluation process, we would have explored in detail the content of the innovative, technology-enriched curriculum and its relevance to the needs of the culturally diverse and changing student population. During step 3, we would have facilitated discussions with the stakeholders to determine how best to disseminate evaluation findings and the lessons learned from the Bunche–Da Vinci evaluation. Furthermore, we would have explored the potential benefits and costs of spending additional resources on hiring another evaluation team to conduct a meta-evaluation of our work.

In the end, I must admit I encountered strong mixed emotions as I worked on this hypothetical case and evaluation plan. As I allowed my imagination to explore fully the context and lives of these students and families, I quickly felt sad and depressed about their conditions and potential plight, but passionate about the need for and opportunity to provide help and external evaluation. As I allowed myself to imagine what could be done using external evaluation if there were no time, resource, and practical constraints, I became elated and appreciative about being trained in evaluation and inspired to apply evaluation as widely as possible. However, this was quickly dampened when I realized I have never encountered a real case in twenty years of practice without time, resource, and practical constraints. My spirits were lowered even more when I imagined the risk of using scarce resources to pay the salaries and expenses of well-educated professionals to provide unnecessary or ineffective evaluation services, when these resources would otherwise be used to educate and help these at-risk students and families. Of course, the beauty of this exercise, just like in a nightmare, is that I would quickly elevate my mood by reminding myself I am dreaming. Now that I (and my colleagues in this volume) have walked this imaginary tightrope with you, I hope you have a better understanding of the value, challenges, and risks of external evaluation. I imagine I do.

References

Alkin, M. C., and Christie, C. A. "An Evaluation Theory Tree." In M. C. Alkin (ed.), *Evaluation Roots*. Thousand Oaks, Calif.: Sage, 2004.

American Evaluation Association. *Guiding Principles for Evaluators.* 2004. http://www.eval.org.

Centers for Disease Control. *Centers for Disease Control Program Evaluation Framework.* Atlanta: Centers for Disease Control, 1999.

Chen, H. T. *Theory-Driven Evaluations*. Thousand Oaks, Calif.: Sage, 1990.

Chen, H. T. "Applying Mixed Methods Under the Framework of Theory-Driven Evaluations." In J. C. Greene and V. J. Caracelli (eds.), *Advances in Mixed-Method Evaluation: The Challenges and Benefits of Integrating Diverse Paradigms*. New Directions for Evaluation, no. 74. San Francisco: Jossey-Bass, 1997.

Chen, H. T. "The Roots of Theory-Driven Evaluation: Current Views and Origins." In M. C. Alkin (ed.), *Evaluation Roots*. Thousand Oaks, Calif.: Sage, 2004.

Chen, H. T. *Practical Program Evaluation: Assessing and Improving Planning, Implementation, and Effectiveness*. Thousand Oaks, Calif.: Sage, 2005.

Donaldson, S. I. "Overcoming Our Negative Reputation: Evaluation Becomes Known as a Helping Profession." *American Journal of Evaluation*, 2001a, 22, 355–361.

Donaldson, S. I. "Mediator and Moderator Analysis in Program Development." In S. Sussman (ed.), *Handbook of Program Development for Health Behavior Research*. Thousand Oaks, Calif.: Sage, 2001b.

Donaldson, S. I. "Theory-Driven Program Evaluation in the New Millennium." In S. I. Donaldson and M. Scriven (eds.), *Evaluating Social Programs and Problems: Visions for the New Millennium*. Mahwah, N.J.: Erlbaum, 2003.

Donaldson, S. I. *Program Theory–Driven Evaluation Science: Strategies and Applications*. Mahwah, N.J.: Erlbaum, forthcoming.

Donaldson, S. I., and Bligh, M. "Rewarding Careers Applying Positive Psychological Science to Improve Quality of Work Life and Organizational Effectiveness." In S. I. Donaldson, D. E. Berger, and K. Pezdek (eds.), *Applied Psychology: New Frontiers and Rewarding Careers*. Mahwah, N.J.: Erlbaum, forthcoming.

Donaldson, S. I., and Christie, C. A. "The 2004 Claremont Debate: Lipsey vs. Scriven: Determining Causality in Program Evaluation and Applied Research: Should Experimental Evidence Be the Gold Standard?" *Journal of Multidisciplinary Evaluation*, forthcoming.

Donaldson, S. I., and Gooler, L. E. "Theory-Driven Evaluation in Action: Lessons from a $20 Million Statewide Work and Health Initiative." *Evaluation and Program Planning,* 2003, *26,* 355–366.

Donaldson, S. I., Gooler, L. E., and Scriven, M. "Strategies for Managing Evaluation Anxiety: Toward a Psychology of Program Evaluation." *American Journal of Evaluation,* 2002, *23*(3), 261–273.

Donaldson, S. I., and Lipsey, M. W. "Roles for Theory in Evaluation Practice." In I. Shaw, J. Greene, and M. Mark (eds.), *Handbook of Evaluation.* Thousand Oaks, Calif.: Sage, forthcoming.

Donaldson, S. I., and Scriven, M. (eds.). *Evaluating Social Programs and Problems: Visions for the New Millennium.* Mahwah, N.J.: Erlbaum, 2003.

Fitzpatrick, J. "Dialog with Stewart Donaldson." *American Journal of Evaluation,* 2002, 23(3), 347–365.

Joint Committee on Standards for Education Evaluation. *The Program Evaluation Standards: How to Assess Evaluations of Educational Programs.* Thousand Oaks, Calif.: Sage, 1994.

Reichhart, C., and Rallis, C. S. (eds.). *The Qualitative-Quantitative Debate: New Perspectives.* New Directions for Program Evaluation, no. 61. San Francisco: Jossey-Bass, 1994.

Rossi, P. H. "My Views of Evaluation and Their Origins." In M. C. Alkin (ed.), *Evaluation Roots.* Thousand Oaks, Calif.: Sage, 2004.

Rossi, P. H., Lipsey, M. W., and Freeman, H. E. *Evaluation: A Systematic Approach.* (7th ed.) Thousand Oaks, Calif.: Sage, 2004.

Scriven, M. "Evaluation in the New Millennium: The Transdisciplinary Vision." In S. I. Donaldson and M. Scriven (eds.), *Evaluating Social Programs and Problems: Visions for the New Millennium.* Mahwah, N.J.: Erlbaum, 2003.

Shadish, W. R., Cook, T. D., and Campbell, D. T. *Experimental and Quasi-Experimental Designs for Generalized Causal Inference.* Boston: Houghton Mifflin, 2002.

Weiss, C. H. *Evaluation: Methods for Studying Programs and Policies.* (2nd ed.) Upper Saddle River, N.J.: Prentice Hall, 1998.

Weiss, C. H. "Rooting for Evaluation: A Cliff Notes Version of My Work." In M. C. Alkin (ed.), *Evaluation Roots.* Thousand Oaks, Calif.: Sage, 2004a.

Weiss, C. H. "On Theory-Based Evaluation: Winning Friends and Influencing People." *Evaluation Exchange,* 2004b, *9*(4), 1–5.

STEWART I. DONALDSON *is dean and professor of psychology at the School of Behavioral and Organizational Sciences, Claremont Graduate University.*

6

The evaluator in this chapter describes potential evaluation capacity-building activities in contrast to the specifics of an evaluation design.

A Proposal to Build Evaluation Capacity at the Bunche–Da Vinci Learning Partnership Academy

Jean A. King

Because my practice is based so thoroughly on what I learn about potential projects interacting with people face-to-face, it is a daunting task to respond to a written evaluation case. Having accepted this challenge, however, I developed a response in three parts: (1) my initial framing of the Bunche–Da Vinci situation, (2) what I would do before signing a contract, and (3) how I might begin the project, knowing that it would inevitably evolve.

An Initial Framing of the Bunche–Da Vinci Evaluation

Matching evaluator to evaluation context is an important issue, so a first consideration is whether I have the appropriate qualifications to conduct this study. Borrowing a distinction that teacher educators use, I would distinguish among three types of knowledge the Bunche–Da Vinci project requires: (1) knowledge of program content (that is, knowledge of elementary urban education partnership programs), (2) knowledge of program evaluation in general, and (3) evaluation content knowledge (that is, knowledge of how to evaluate elementary urban education partnership programs). Using this tripart analysis, I feel confident that I am qualified to conduct the study:

• *Program content knowledge.* I began my career as a seventh-grade English teacher and have worked in public education settings for over thirty years. A decade ago I studied two innovative urban schools in the Twin

Cities in Minnesota and spent a number of years as co-coordinator of an urban professional development school. I have a general understanding of literacy and numeracy issues in elementary schools and have participated in several educational collaborations.

• *Program evaluation knowledge.* I have been a program evaluator for roughly twenty-five years and hold a lifetime Class A Evaluator's license from the state of Louisiana. I direct an evaluation studies program for a research university and write regularly about evaluation issues.

• *Evaluation content knowledge.* I have participated on teams evaluating several urban education programs, including projects involving both elementary schools and collaborations. From 1999 to 2002, I served as the research and evaluation coordinator for a large school district where I directed several relevant evaluations (including an elementary literacy project and a graduation standards review) that provide direct correlates for this new setting. The Bunche–Da Vinci opportunity would be of particular interest to me because I enjoy collaborating with teachers and administrators on school-level projects.

What evaluation theory would I bring to bear at Bunche–Da Vinci? For the faculty and administration, mandated high-stakes accountability testing has focused attention as never before on their abilities to increase student achievement and scores on two standardized tests. They are well aware that their school's successes and failures are fodder for stories in the media and are on notice to improve, dramatically and quickly. In part because of new technology that makes relevant data accessible, they have within their reach the prospect of creating an infrastructure to support evaluation activities. Given my commitment to long-term improvement in urban school settings, I would reframe the principal's request for evaluation to one for evaluation capacity building (ECB), that is, "intentional work to constantly co-create and co-sustain an overall process that makes quality evaluation and its uses routine in organizations and systems" (Stockdill, Baizerman, and Compton, 2002, p. 14). Mary García would have to be interested in this approach. Knowing the political risk of such an endeavor, I might also ask Superintendent Chase and the study's foundation sponsor to sign off as well.

Compton, Glover-Kudon, Smith, and Avery (2002) distinguish between evaluation practice and ECB practice. For "the ECB practitioner . . . the focus . . . was first on responding to requests for evaluation services while simultaneously considering how today's work will contribute to sustaining the unit in the longer term" (p. 55). I would argue that it makes good sense to invest the resources available to develop an infrastructure for continued evaluative activity at Bunche–Da Vinci. My framing question would be: What can I do as an evaluator to collaborate with the Bunche–Da Vinci community to create an environment that will support an ongoing process of evaluation and the integral use of its results? Years ago I adapted the Schwab commonplaces of a learning situation (teacher, students, curriculum, and milieu) to evaluation: the evaluator serves as teacher, the users as students, the evaluation process and results as "curriculum," and the evaluation context as the milieu (Schwab, 1969; King and Thompson, 1983). My goal at Bunche–Da Vinci would be instructional: to connect with the principal, faculty, and staff (and others as appropriate) both to teach evaluation processes and facilitate people's use of the results we generate. Once García agreed, my goal would be to collaborate with Bunche–Da Vinci staff to increase the likelihood that an evaluation process could continue within the school. Evaluation capacity building means using this process not only for its immediate and direct results, but also for the explicit purpose of building participants' personal capacity to evaluate again. (Some may see ECB practice as a branch of the "use" limb of Alkin's evaluation theory tree, that is, a natural extension of utilization-focused evaluation; Patton, 1997. Others, who hold the act of valuing as the unique and necessary role of the evaluator, may be unwilling to label this work evaluation at all, labeling it instead a distinct practice—a sapling sprouting near the theory tree.) The evaluator plays an important quality control role.

The ECB approach to knowledge construction will necessarily involve mixed paradigms and methods at Bunche–Da Vinci. On the one hand, García wants to install a number of new systems (teacher collaboration, monitoring curriculum and instruction, student interventions, and communication), each of which will need to be monitored as it is implemented. Descriptive data will document what is taking place and people's perceptions of the changes. Such data may also answer Superintendent Chase's questions about the manageability of the Da Vinci curriculum. On the other hand, the superintendent knows that García needs a reliable source of evaluative data on the impact of the program or parts of it. It would therefore make sense to compile existing quantitative student achievement data to make sense of them, working to understand why the internal Da Vinci scores differ so dramatically from the state test scores and what teachers might do about that, the second of the superintendent's concerns. The creation of an in-school database for compiling and using achievement data is an essential first step. Absent this, the faculty and staff will continue their work unable to use the available standardized benchmarks easily.

Before Signing a Contract

Before I put pen to evaluation contract, I would engage in two important activities, which I call *reconnoitering* and *negotiating*. The purpose of reconnoitering (one might also call it surveying or scouting) is to learn as much as I can about the proposed evaluation setting and the key actors within it. If possible (assuming I did not already know), I would check with my professional network of trusted contacts in both the Bunche–Da Vinci school district and other nearby districts to find out as much as possible about topics like the following: (1) what people think is really happening at the school, (2) the style and reputation of Chase and García, (3) local school board politics that might be affecting the collaboration, and (4) the district's interest in and commitment to program evaluation, as opposed to standardized testing. Related to this final topic, I would want to learn about the district's Testing (or Research or Evaluation or Assessment) Department (its name alone would provide valuable information) and its ability to generate and maintain good data, the accessibility of data to schools, the effect of No Child Left Behind, the department's role in school improvement planning in the district, and so on. I would also want to understand the role the state department of education plays in district accountability activities.

Because this project is likely to be high profile, I would also conduct informal research in three areas. First, I would go online and check available information on student achievement at the school and comparable schools. (In Minnesota, a great deal of information is available on the state's department of education Web site; one can spend hours making comparisons.) Second, I would use a search engine to find information about the Da Vinci Learning Corporation and read both its Web material and any commentary on it in an effort to determine its status and reputation. I might also phone or email colleagues who would know more than me about the corporation's work. Third, I would do a quick literature review on programs similar to this collaboration. This would not be an extensive search but enough to place the program in a research context, helping me know what existing research has suggested about such efforts.

The second important activity prior to signing the contract is the act of negotiating. I would first have to clarify who exactly is the client. Is it Mary García, Douglas Chase, someone else from the district office, or some combination of the above? Who will be the primary intended users? What roles will parents and community members play, if any? The school board? What about representatives from the Da Vinci Learning Corporation, who have much at stake here? The study's time line is another important concern. I would hope for a three- to five-year time frame since we will be examining things that do not quickly change. What is a realistic time line? Can the contract cover more than an initial year? The answers to these questions might well affect the emphasis placed on certain of the questions raised.

Regardless of the client, however, I would advocate six nonnegotiable items:

1. An evaluation team of at least two and possibly more, ensuring the inclusion of people with the following attributes: at least one evaluator of Hispanic background who is fluent in Spanish, someone who has taught in a similar program, someone knowledgeable about evaluating collaborations, and someone with expertise in educational testing and statistical analysis. (The DGHK team is a solid beginning, but does not include all of the background needed.)

2. The active involvement of school-based participants. I would propose a collaborative study with the intent of building evaluation capacity through a purposeful evaluation training function. This requires regularly scheduled meetings, assignments for some internal staff, and repeated interaction with the evaluation team, far beyond what might be demanded in a more evaluator-directed study. Not every site is interested in such an approach, and given the reportedly negative attitudes of many teachers, this may not be possible at Bunche–Da Vinci.

3. A formal process to ensure regular reflection with school faculty and staff about how the evaluation capacity building is proceeding.

4. The flexibility to change course as needed throughout the study and a collaborative process for making decisions to change.

5. Required communication during the project to key stakeholders and stakeholder groups, including (1) individual meetings (for example, with the superintendent or Da Vinci leadership) as necessary; (2) oral and short written reports to key groups throughout the project, sometimes involving school staff as presenters; and (3) a mutually agreed-on final report appropriate to the setting (which is to say, there may not be a lengthy technical document prepared at the study's end).

6. Sufficient support for the project, including fees for the evaluators, incentives for faculty and staff participation (selected from the following list: stipends, materials, release time, reduced teaching load, conference attendance, refreshments), and required materials (for example, flip chart paper, copying, and computer software).

Also I would suggest that Mary García and I develop proposed outcomes for the project, beginning with the following list:

1. Knowledge about how well the components of her new system are being implemented, how they are working, and what, if any, improvements might be needed

2. Understanding why Da Vinci test scores and the state test scores differ so dramatically

3. Understanding the recent years' state test scores and, if possible, their direct implications for instruction within the school

4. The creation of a formal system and structures for evaluation (by whatever name) within Bunche–Da Vinci, including tackling school-based instructional issues, collecting and compiling data, and reflecting on what might be done

5. Increased evaluation knowledge and skills in-house (for example, understanding how to analyze and interpret test results, having a sense of what to do about a low score in a given area)

6. Positive attitudes toward evaluation in the school (that is, faculty and staff report liking evaluation, or at least not dreading it)

García and I would revise these together prior to my signing a contract, including Chase and any other primary intended users in the conversation as appropriate. We would therefore begin the study with a clear agreement on what we plan to create by its completion.

Collaborating with Bunche–Da Vinci Staff to Build Evaluation Capacity

It is one thing to negotiate a successful contract; it is another thing altogether to conduct a successful collaboration in a complex and changing environment like Bunche–Da Vinci. My experience in similar school settings has suggested five key activities that can help develop a culture of evaluation and increase evaluation capacity: (1) creating an evaluation advisory group, (2) beginning to build a formal evaluation infrastructure, (3) making sense of test scores, (4) conducting one highly visible participatory inquiry, and (5) instituting action research activities. I would propose working on these, staged over several years, knowing that every single one will take much longer than I imagine and will evolve as people bring it to life in this context. It is to be expected that some activities will go better than others, but the ongoing reflection process will enable us to make revisions as needed.

Creating an Evaluation Advisory Committee. Since García is serious about studying the proposed changes, I would invite her to establish a small, but compatible Evaluation Advisory Committee (EAC), initially consisting of herself and two or three positive-minded opinion leaders from the faculty. This small group would be the initial primary intended users of the evaluation process, what I sometimes call (though hating the negative image) the evaluation "virus" that potentially will "infect" the school's professional community with positive evaluation thinking. (Each time I use this image with clients, I emphasize its unfortunate negativity. I sometimes use the image of yeast, but that too has potentially negative connotations.) The committee will charge itself with several activities; members will collaboratively help design studies, monitor evaluation activities, get firsthand feedback from data users, and so on. Through regular meetings, they are the heart of the reflection process. Committee membership will be flexible—people will come and go—and is likely to evolve as people's lives and schedules change.

My experience suggests that this committee needs four different types of members, often embodied in just a few individuals:

Staff who are highly respected and truly know the school's culture and inhabitants well. These are individuals who have excellent interpersonal skills (including the intuition to pick up on people's affect), who have likely taught at Bunche–Da Vinci a few years, and who can readily learn what their colleagues are really thinking because people freely talk to them.

People who understand evaluation and enjoy data. In my experience, there are individuals in every school who enjoy the evaluation process, either because they understand it intuitively and are eager to learn more or because they have had formal training, typically in a degree program. They often admit this attribute sheepishly, knowing that many will label it surprising.

Those positive "can do" individuals who can get things done efficiently and thoughtfully.

At least one person with a good sense of humor who will remind the group that this work should be agreeable, even at its most challenging, and that an occasional smile or chuckle is a good thing.

Would I include naysayers on this initial committee? Some think that including negative individuals in the initial steps of a change process will give diverse perspectives to committee discussions, encourage them to get with the program, and support the notion of representative democracy in the school community. To my mind, these folks are rarely helpful and may dismantle or demoralize an otherwise enthusiastic group. I advise not including negative people in this initial group. This does not mean, however, that you ignore them; the advisory committee must attend to their interests and concerns individually and extremely purposefully or they may shut the process down.

Since conflict is inherent in the evaluation process, the conceptual framing for the EAC's work is that of the dual concerns model for understanding conflict (Johnson, 1997). Deutsch's classic model reminds us that people in conflict have two important concerns: reaching a goal (in this case, conducting meaningful evaluation activities) and simultaneously maintaining relationships (Deutsch, 1949). Collaborative problem solving and negotiation is the process that facilitates both goal attainment and positive relationships (there are four other processes that are less effective), so my job as evaluator would be to help the members of the EAC engage in collaborative problem solving as we move through the evaluation process. It is this group that would, over time, take on the broad evaluation question related to instruction at Bunche–Da Vinci, the challenging effort of determining what exactly "the" instructional program is and what its effects are. I would take responsibility for integrating that into the longitudinal EAC activities once I was confident that the committee was functioning effectively.

Beginning to Build an Evaluation Infrastructure. The EAC marks the first step in creating an evaluation infrastructure for Bunche–Da Vinci. Once formed, it will be charged with responsibility for two types of activities: (1) studying the school's context to determine the availability of certain infrastructure requirements and (2) directly taking other actions to build the infrastructure.

Assessing the Context. Over the initial months, I would propose focusing on three areas of the evaluation context. First, we would be well advised to make sense of the accountability context in which the school finds itself at both the state and the district levels. Accountability requirements, driven by federal No Child Left Behind and state mandates, require that the school produce certain types of data routinely, and our infrastructure must allow for this in addition to any other targeted evaluation efforts we might propose. It would also be important to assess the district accountability environment to determine possible interest in—or opposition to—the EAC's activities. If the external environment for whatever reason is not likely to support potential data-based changes, García and her staff need to know sooner rather than later.

A second area of context requiring immediate examination is that of decision making. First—and García may well know the answer to this question—what is senior administration's interest in and demand for evaluation information? To what extent does Superintendent Chase want to be involved in the study, in tracking its progress or hearing its results? Given the central administration's ability to change the course of the Bunche–Da Vinci partnership dramatically, this grounding is important knowledge. Second, is there a feedback mechanism in place that will effectively position the results of this evaluation into decision-making processes at both the district and the school levels? Absent such a mechanism, the group may have to create one. Third, will school teachers and staff have sufficient autonomy in their decision making? In other words, will people truly be able to act on data, or will some structure external to the school limit actions in certain areas? For example, is the Da Vinci curriculum carved in stone? If data suggest it could be improved, will teachers be able to make changes? The committee needs to understand the bounds within which teachers and staff must operate.

A third and final topic for study in the context is access to resources. If resources are available, the capacity-building effort is enhanced; if not, then the time line may be significantly slowed or even made impossible. These resources are of two types:

• *Access to evaluation and research knowledge and training.* If school staff want to build evaluation capacity, then access to evaluation knowledge (for example, data analysis, interpreting test scores, research bases) is essential. Access to evaluation and research knowledge typically includes access to people—district evaluation personnel, other external consultants, or even volunteers (such as faculty or students from a local university engaged in a service learning effort)—who can explain evaluation. It may also include access to information on evaluation resources (for example, Web sites, books, evaluation reports, tools) or access to either formal training or informal coaching on evaluation processes. The staff already have access to me and others on the evaluation team, and we would be eager to teach people.

• *Access to district resources to support the evaluation process at Bunche–Da Vinci.* Beyond basic resources like copying, computers, and data printouts, this includes fiscal support from the central or building administration to provide, for example, time within the workday to collaborate on evaluation activities (for example, by providing substitute teachers to free people from classroom responsibilities), funds to buy a meal if a group works into the evening, or honoraria for faculty or staff who commit to participating extensively in the evaluation process. My experience over the course of the past decade suggests that although teachers truly value time to collaborate during the school day, they perceive missing class (preparing for a substitute teacher and then dealing with the effects of being gone) as far more costly than working after school, in the evening, or on weekends. This creates a difficult quandary for building evaluation capacity.

Building the Infrastructure Directly. In addition to assessing the context, the EAC, with the evaluation team's assistance, would begin work on activities to increase the evaluation infrastructure directly in the internal organizational context and thus to create an appropriate conception of evaluation for Bunche–Da Vinci. They are fortunate in that there is already supportive leadership at the building (the principal, who will clearly champion this cause) and at the district office (the superintendent), a necessary component in my experience. The committee would directly seek to improve the school climate, making it supportive of change through evaluation. They would do this by their positive attitudes toward evaluation, their open-mindedness when challenged, their respect for colleagues' opinions, their enthusiasm for risk taking and creativity, and a continuing sense of good humor. Committee members would become evaluation champions, serving as visible supporters of the process, mentioning it in favorable terms, identifying issues for possible study, and taking on naysayers pleasantly but firmly throughout the school day and across the school year.

The committee would establish three structures to teach the evaluation process. First, we would collaboratively develop an explicit plan and realistic time line for building evaluation capacity at Bunche–Da Vinci. Such a plan would include the following content:

Rewriting school policies and procedures to include core evaluation capacity–building principles (for example, the expectation that routine activities related to school improvement activities will be evaluated annually, routine compilation and discussion of data related to core activities, explicit evaluative roles for committee chairs).

Creating opportunities for faculty and staff (and, over time, students and parents) to collaborate and participate in various ways on evaluation activities and then, with the group's support, mandating them as appropriate. One way to facilitate this, borrowed from social psychology, is to create interdependent roles whereby people necessarily support each other in completing evaluation tasks.

Developing formal mechanisms for reflection on data. It would be helpful to create peer learning structures through which teachers and other staff could come together routinely to reflect on evaluation data.

Second, based on resources available for the task, the EAC would decide how to build a within-school infrastructure to support the technical components of the evaluation process. This is necessary to ensure the accuracy of data collected and the efficiency of the process. The infrastructure would include a variety of processes, such as an occasional process to measure needs; a mechanism to frame questions and generate studies; and a way to design evaluations, collect, analyze, and interpret data, and report results both internally in the school community and to the wider public.

Third, the committee would create a structure to socialize faculty and staff purposefully into the organization's evaluation process, both initially and over time. There would be clear expectations that everyone is expected (or even required) to "do" evaluation (the stick) and equally clear incentives for participation (carrots). The EAC would also structure ways for those interested to receive training in evaluation through informal workshops at the school or formal courses offered in the community. To the extent that Bunche–Da Vinci staff teach and have their offices near one another and regularly socialize during the workday (for example, sharing meals and snacks), evaluation socializing will be easier. The committee might also need to consider trust-building activities in the short term, given the perceived dissension in the ranks.

Establishing the EAC and beginning to work on the evaluation infrastructure would mark an important beginning. In that critical first year or two, I would also propose three key activities to engage people and model the evaluation process: making sense of test scores, conducting at least one highly visible participatory study, and laying the groundwork for eventual action research efforts by groups of faculty and staff. Ideally, a different member of the committee in collaboration with a member of the evaluation team would lead each of these efforts. Other members of the school community—such as faculty, staff, parents, and district office staff—would participate and learn alongside. It is likely that the resources (especially time) to do all three activities might well be lacking, and we might plan to stage these over several years. But I would want people to understand how these could help make the evaluation process meaningful in the lives of faculty and staff and, potentially, parents and students. Absent meaningful examples, administrators, teachers, staff, and community residents alike may never move from intuitive evaluation to systematic efforts.

Key Activity 1: Making Sense of Test Scores. The importance of this activity cannot be overstated. American education currently lives in an environment laden with accountability measures (some call this "accountabilism"), and the failure to make sense of the Bunche–Da Vinci test scores could quickly lead to additional internal dismay and public humiliation. I would therefore propose that one or two members of the EAC agree to lead a separate committee that would be charged with studying the school's test scores—both company and state—for the past several years and interpreting them with a view to action. We would access someone (from the evaluation team, the district office, a local university, or research shop) with a good understanding of test interpretation and, ideally, the ability to work with the data to answer targeted questions the group might raise. How helpful this activity will be in relation to specific actions teachers can take in their classrooms depends greatly on the content of the tests and the quality of the existing data. Regardless, it could lead to the development of a functional database that teachers could access for information on their current students. This would be an important development for the use of student data and, hence, for evaluation capacity building.

This committee might develop program theory that would plan backward from the necessary achievement outcomes to identify explicit strategies to increase learning in specific areas. Again, the assistance of an outside expert in student learning could be extremely helpful. We might choose to conduct meetings with small groups (perhaps teachers at given grade levels, language arts teachers across grades, and so on) to process the data.

Key Activity 2: Conducting One Highly Visible Participatory Inquiry. Modeling the evaluation process for the school community is one way to demonstrate how to frame an evaluation question, develop instruments, collect and analyze data, and then make recommendations. I used this process when I served as research and evaluation coordinator for a large school district, systematically teaching participants in the course of three studies on topics that mattered greatly to people (high school graduation standards, special education, and proposed changes in the middle schools). People participated and paid close attention because they truly cared about the outcomes.

At Bunche–Da Vinci, the obvious topic for the initial study would be the implementation of García's new systems for teacher collaboration, monitoring curriculum and instruction (including the manageability of the Da Vinci curriculum), student interventions, and communication. Such an effort would be a classic example of evaluation process use—we would be studying the systems as they were being created, which is developmental evaluation at its best. I would propose a participatory evaluation process involving a team of twenty to twenty-five people—representatives of teachers, staff, perhaps parents, perhaps students, Da Vinci representatives, district representatives, our evaluation team, and, if available, university professors. This collaborative team would meet monthly throughout the course of the year, and the EAC representative, with support from the evaluation team, would meet in between to prepare materials for the next month's meeting. Together, the group would identify stakeholder concerns, develop evaluation questions and credible methods, help develop instruments, analyze and interpret data, and collaboratively make recommendations. The evaluation team and EAC would provide expertise and oversight, respectively.

In my experience, the participants in such a study become close while simultaneously gaining a sense of how program evaluation works. If the process were successful, I might later encourage the EAC to form a group to examine the effects of computer-assisted instruction since several parents have already expressed concern and might form the natural core of a second study committee.

Key Activity 3: Instituting Action Research Activities—or at Least Planting the Seeds. I have never succeeded in bringing this final activity fully to life anywhere I have collaborated, but it remains one of my intentions when I work in partnership with a school community. The ideal would be for groups of collaborating teachers and staff to institute action research efforts on specific interventions with specific students to raise test scores, for example, first-grade teachers working with students struggling with letter recognition or fourth-grade staff whose students have low scores on their Da Vinci standardized test on a certain topic. The action research cycle—plan, act, observe, and reflect—is intuitive; good teachers will note that they informally engage in it every day. What I would propose is making the process more explicit and public as a means of addressing instructional improvement directly.

Teachers would meet and identify extremely specific instructional activities that they know or believe are effective ("promising practices") to teach this skill. They would agree to try out a strategy, measure the results, and then meet in a month to discuss what happened (Schmoker, 1999). In contrast to the second key activity, the highly visible study that models evaluation collaboration, these would be fairly private studies that model how individual teachers can facilitate targeted learning of specific individuals. Action research could also be a method to monitor the curriculum, one of the superintendent's concerns, or for an annual data-based school improvement process. Although difficult to institute and sustain, action research can provide visible and transparent results, a way to share and reflect on them, and hence bring the evaluation process to life within classrooms, a clear component of evaluation capacity building. In my judgment, the EAC would want to develop a process that includes training in collaborative teamwork, an opportunity for people to identify their own burning issues, incentives for participation, and a structure that would enable projects to be completed in a reasonable time frame. Supporting these action research projects might be an additional role for members of the evaluation team.

Planning for evaluation capacity building differs from planning for an evaluation. Rather than developing an evaluation design in a traditional sense, I have presented a list of activities in this section that would foster a culture of evaluation: creating an evaluation advisory group, beginning to build a formal evaluation infrastructure, making sense of test scores, conducting one highly visible participatory inquiry, and instituting action research activities. In conjunction with the evaluation team, the teachers, administrators, and staff of Bunche–Da Vinci would take responsibility for designing evaluative activities they believe would make a difference for the school. Given the life of an elementary school, it is inconceivable that we would tackle every one of these tasks simultaneously, even if we had considerable resources. The ongoing collaboration between the EAC and the evaluation team would, however, yield decisions on next steps on a continuing basis to—if I may use another bad metaphor—fan the flames of the evaluation capacity–building fire. Building momentum is key, and it is hard to overcome negative attitudes and inertia in a school culture where people may perceive program evaluation as an unnatural act. Throughout, I would maintain close contact with members of the EAC as the primary creators and users of the evaluation processes at Bunche–Da Vinci and with my evaluation teammates, who would be working on various components of the project.

Ever the optimist, I begin each evaluation with eyes open to a situation's possibilities. I would not want to participate otherwise. On the positive side, the Bunche–Da Vinci study offers a rare opportunity: to engage the professional community of an urban elementary school in an evaluation process that holds the potential to improve instructional practice dramatically and, with it, student learning. I would collaborate with people who have chosen to work in a school setting that I value, top leadership at both the building and district endorse the effort and appear likely to use its results, sufficient resources are available to support evaluation activities, and political issues seem navigable—at least at the outset. I would jump at the chance.

References

Compton, D., Glover-Kudon, R., Smith, I. E., and Avery, M. E. "Ongoing Capacity Building in the American Cancer Society (ACS), 1995–2001." In D. W. Compton, M. Baizerman, and S. H. Stockdill (eds.), *The Art, Craft, and Science of Evaluation Capacity Building.* New Directions for Evaluation, no. 93. San Francisco: Jossey-Bass, 2002.

Deutsch, M. "A Theory of Cooperation and Competition upon Group Process." *Human Relations,* 1949, 2, 199–231.

Johnson, D. W. *Reaching Out: Interpersonal Effectiveness and Self-Actualization.* Needham Heights, Mass.: Allyn and Bacon, 1997.

King, J. A., and Thompson, B. "Research on School Use of Program Evaluation: A Literature Review and Research Agenda." *Studies in Educational Evaluation,* 1983, 9, 5–21.

Patton, M. Q. *Utilization-Focused Evaluation.* (3rd ed.) Thousand Oaks, Calif.: Sage, 1997.

Schmoker, M. *Results: The Key to Continuous School Improvement.* (2nd ed.) Alexandria, Va.: Association for Supervision and Curriculum Development, 1999.

Schwab, J. "The Practical: A Language for Curriculum." *School Review,* 1969, 78(1), 1–23.

Stockdill, S. H., Baizerman, M., and Compton, D. "Toward a Definition of the ECB Process: A Conversation with the ECB Literature." In D. W. Compton, M. Baizerman, and S. H. Stockdill (eds.), *The Art, Craft, and Science of Evaluation Capacity Building.* New Directions for Evaluation, no. 93. San Francisco: Jossey-Bass, 2002.

JEAN A. KING *is a professor at the University of Minnesota, where she coordinates the Evaluation Studies Program in the Department of Educational Policy and Administration.*

7

The editors give each of the theorists a chance to respond to questions posed about the context of the situation in relation to their own experience in the field, exploring how the exercise had an impact on their evaluation designs.

The Reality of Unreal Situations: Caveats and Insights

Marvin C. Alkin, Christina A. Christie, Jennifer C. Greene, Gary T. Henry, Stewart I. Donaldson, Jean A. King

The specifics of the case (the context) are highly important to how different theorists will react in conducting an evaluation. By this, we think of contexts in a very broad sense. A context is not only a disciplinary field (say, education) or a specific kind of program within that field (Head Start, for example), but also all the particularities that relate to the organization, the individuals within that organization, and those who are affected by the program. The context is also influenced by how broadly the evaluator chooses to view the program.

In the instance of Bunche–Da Vinci, we have an elementary school in a low-income, heavily bilingual area. We also have a program that is a unique partnership of the school and the Da Vinci Learning Corporation. Each of the theorists has done evaluations related to education, though not necessarily elementary schools. The four theorists admittedly have differential levels of experience in dealing with instances like Bunche–Da Vinci. King and Greene have had the most firsthand experience with situations like that presented to them. Henry has dealt with the evaluation of educational programs, but within the context of public policy. Thus, his experience with evaluating education is at a more macro level. Donaldson has performed evaluations in a variety of fields, with his primary exposure to education outside the context of K–12. What impact does this have on the way in which the theorists deal with Bunche–Da Vinci?

The way this exercise was constructed also has implications for how the theorists might approach the evaluation. Some theoretical approaches are simply less compatible with this exercise. Some evaluators might feel uncomfortable with being commissioned by a school principal to perform an evaluation of the program. Some might desire to work with higher-level administration to ensure that the evaluation is directed at someone with the authority to make decisions. Others might find it inimical to conduct an evaluation in which there is not initial broad stakeholder involvement. Thus, it is clear that the evaluation theorists' responses in the previous chapters represent but a single instance of how they might implement an evaluation, and the parameters of the scenario may have constrained their ability to explicate their approaches fully.

To examine the extent to which the context of this exercise and the exercise itself had an impact on the products produced by the four theorists, we posed the following four questions for their response:

1. What information did you see as missing from the case, and what major assumptions did you make in the absence of that information?
2. How similar (or dissimilar) is the setting described in the case to those in which you typically conduct evaluations?
3. To what extent can the evaluation proposed in your chapter be viewed as fully explicative of your approach?
4. What is your assessment of the likelihood that you would be able to implement and complete the evaluation as you have described it?

Responses

What information did you see as missing from the case, and what major assumptions did you make in the absence of that information?

JENNIFER C. GREENE: There was insufficient information on the educational, organizational, and political context of the school district and its urban setting. Urban school districts are enormously complex settings, with their own internal political challenges and the external demands of accountability adding considerable pressure to those in charge. I made few assumptions about these dimensions of the Bunche–Da Vinci evaluation context. Instead, I concentrated on the smaller context of the school, assuming that Mary García as the principal had the authority and responsibility to act without extensive consultation with district authorities.

Also missing was information about the Da Vinci Learning Corporation and about the theory and logic of its program for "low-performing schools." In this regard, I assumed the corporation was to be a minor player in the evaluation. And I held the theory of the program up for evaluative scrutiny and critique.

It was also very difficult to get a sense of the school community—the life of the school's neighborhoods and their residents. Particularly perplexing was the apparent mobility of the neighborhoods and the mobility of the students in the school, juxtaposed with reported parent and student satisfaction with the school. Especially, who are the Spanish-speaking families coming into the community and the school? Are they recent immigrants or people moving from elsewhere? From what Spanish-speaking countries do they originate? How homogeneous or heterogeneous is this particular community? And so forth. My evaluation design did not assume these were central issues in the school but did include and attend to them.

Furthermore, there was little information on the legal parameters of the public-private partnership that was the Bunche–Da Vinci Learning Academy. I assumed this was worthy of further investigation and critique in the evaluation.

GARY T. HENRY: At first, I was stymied by the single school focus of the description. After thinking more deeply about the circumstances, I realized that many of the questions that García and Chase would find compelling were most likely to be comparative and that the philanthropies were likely to be interested in the learning model as well as Bunche–Da Vinci Academy. Since the evaluations that I have done are statewide and comparative, and generally include counterfactuals, elevating the evaluation's focus made the proposal more similar to evaluations that I have done.

Rather than make assumptions, I developed a comprehensive approach to the evaluation. The proposal contains almost all of the elements that I would frequently include in an evaluation, although rarely am I able to include all four in a single evaluation proposal. They are likely to be sequential, which is consistent with the proposal, but often they are funded separately.

STEWART I. DONALDSON: The most notable challenge I encountered was not being able to ascertain and verify information from dynamic interactions with the stakeholders. This forced me to use a new and untested evaluation method to make decisions: my imagination. I highlighted many of the major assumptions I needed to make in order to illustrate more fully my approach. I think the more subtle central assumptions I made included the assumption that García and Chase would allow us the time and access to meet with the diverse stakeholders to discuss the program and evaluation. I also assumed they were truly interested in objective external evaluation, and not just planning to use my evaluation to support decisions they had already made, personal agendas, or as a way to find data that could be used to justify terminating the contract with their corporate partner.

JEAN A. KING: There are at least two categories of critical unknowns in the setting that would raise my interpersonal antennas and make me ever vigilant to signs of trouble. First are the uncertainties of this evaluation's client and the role that district politics may unavoidably play at Bunche–Da Vinci, regardless of what we accomplish within the school. Numerous questions spring to mind: How long will Superintendent Chase give free rein to Mary García and her reform efforts? How actively are school board members involved with the school, and how do they perceive its situation? To what extent will the nationally conspicuous collaboration with Da Vinci affect changes the school might propose? How viable is the Da Vinci collaboration to begin with? What is the district's budget situation in the coming years?

Second are the multiple uncertainties related to the school itself and to the people who work there: the instructional program as implemented, the details of the principal's proposed and enacted changes, the depth of discontent among the faculty and staff, García's leadership capabilities, the realities of the community (for example, historical tensions, leadership, and other assets available), and so on. The project would likely demand a great deal of presence on-site to resolve these uncertainties and address the conflicts or dilemmas arising from them. My chapter assumed that the principal agreed to evaluation capacity building using a participatory process over time and that none of these issues would interfere with the evaluation process. In all likelihood, unknown elements will unavoidably affect the process in ways that can be understood only as they develop.

2. How similar (or dissimilar) is the setting described in the case to those in which you typically conduct evaluations?

JENNIFER C. GREENE: I am very familiar with public school K–12 settings, including schools in underserved and underresourced settings. I have conducted many evaluation projects in our nation's public schools, and my graduate education is in the field of education. Thus, I bring considerable experience and understanding to a public K–12 evaluation context. I am deeply concerned about the well-being of marginalized people in our society and about the inequities and injustices they continue to suffer. And I have devoted time to thinking about how evaluation can be best positioned to serve the interests of such people. I am most committed to *public* programs and policies that concern our national priorities and our democratic commitments. Thus, in multiple ways, the Bunche–Da Vinci scenario is a good match to my experience and sensibilities as an evaluator.

GARY T. HENRY: After shifting from the single school to a comparison of schools using the learning model, the setting was reasonably similar to those in which I frequently work. In most cases, I am interested in evaluating interventions that are intended to improve educational performance and I am always focused on outcomes. So with a sleight of hand to elevate the focus and make it comparative, the setting became comfortable for me and the type of evaluation I usually conduct.

STEWART I. DONALDSON: My career has involved evaluation adventures into many diverse settings and contexts. For example, I have worked on evaluations in a variety of education, corporate, university, public health, health care, community, and nonprofit settings. While I have never encountered a case exactly like Bunche–Da Vinci and do not specialize in K–12 evaluation, many features of this case seemed familiar. Namely, I have recently evaluated technology-enriched curricula and measured student performance, evaluated educational programs for ethnically and culturally diverse bilingual youth living in low-income and impoverished conditions, and worked on evaluations that engaged school and corporate administrators. I would certainly agree this is not a typical case for me, but I did not feel I was a complete stranger to the context or at a loss for predicting issues and challenges that would likely emerge.

JEAN A. KING: I have worked in urban school settings for many years although more commonly at the secondary level than the elementary, so the Bunche–Da Vinci setting would be fairly typical for me. One small consequence of the No Child Left Behind legislation, with its emphasis on standardized testing, which often trumps program evaluation in districts, has been to move my evaluation practice beyond schools. The general process of capacity building applies to these differing contexts well; the contexts affect how it develops over time.

3. To what extent can the evaluation proposed in your chapter be viewed as fully explicative of your approach?

JENNIFER C. GREENE: The proposed evaluation reflects my views on evaluation to a significant extent. It captures much of what I believe is important in evaluation practice. This includes active and explicit engagement with critical values in evaluation (contextuality, inclusion, learning and education, diversity and difference, and the public good); an emphasis on the meaningfulness of lived experience, or on the program as experienced in context by various stakeholders; attention to the relational dimensions of being an evaluator and especially to the character of respect and reciprocity therein; and an understanding of evaluation as a moral and ethical practice, in and of itself.

Some of my other evaluation commitments and predispositions did not get as much airtime as I would have ideally liked. These include the following. First, the evaluation design I proposed does include a mix of methods and methodological perspectives. But this mix is not as thoughtful and therefore not as powerful as it potentially could be. Particularly in politically challenging contexts, a thoughtful mix of methods can provide an important avenue for respectful and meaningful engagement with varied perspectives and interests. This could be very useful in the Bunche–Da Vinci context. Second, the evaluation design I proposed pays insufficient attention to these internal politics, particularly to the interests and concerns of important players in district and corporate politics. In the value-engaged approach I am promoting in this volume, the value of inclusion means inclusion of not only the marginalized but also those currently in power, as their concerns are also important and legitimate. The design overlooked, even neglected, the interests of the powerful. Third, I believe that theory-oriented perspectives on evaluation are also useful and potentially powerful. These were underused in this design.

GARY T. HENRY: The main assumption that was necessary was that the principal and the superintendent would be interested in comparative data about the implementation and effectiveness of the Da Vinci Learning Model. I would like to have better understood why parents preferred this school but complained about the focus of the instruction and emphasis on technology. I also wondered about the absence of district personnel and district-initiated activities.

STEWART I. DONALDSON: My approach has evolved, and continues to evolve, in response to developments in the discipline and practice of evaluation and my cumulative experiences practicing evaluation science. The approach I described and used in this volume reflects my current thinking about a rather specific but substantial slice of evaluation practice. I refer to this domain as program effectiveness evaluation (Fitzpatrick, 2002), which involves evaluating a program under real versus ideal conditions. I distinguish this from program efficacy evaluation, or evaluating a program under ideal or research-like conditions. In my view, many of the contemporary debates and even texts in evaluation do not make this distinction clear enough. It is very common to observe program effectiveness evaluations being designed with, or judged by, program efficacy evaluation methods and standards.

I have developed my approach to program evaluation so that it can be widely used and adapted to both worlds: program efficacy and effectiveness evaluation. I have used program theory–driven science employing randomized control trials to evaluate program efficacy (Donaldson, Graham, and Hansen, 1994) and to isolate harmful side effects of programs implemented in public and private elementary and intermediate school settings (Donaldson, Graham, Piccinin, and Hansen, 1995). I have also used program theory–driven evaluation science in a wide range of program effectiveness evaluation projects (for example, see Donaldson and Gooler, 2003). I believe one of the most desirable features of this program evaluation approach is that it promises to bridge the divide between social and evaluation scientists evaluating program efficacy (see Lipsey and Wilson, 1993), and the work of evaluation practitioners typically conducting program effectiveness evaluations. The proposed Bunche–Da Vinci evaluation is intended to be explicative of how I would approach a program effectiveness evaluation based on the information I was provided and the assumptions I made.

JEAN A. KING: The chapter I wrote in response to the case accurately details my current evaluation approach. I believe so strongly in collaboration that I will not typically take a job in which clients request what I would call an evaluator-driven evaluation, that is, where the evaluator (or external evaluation team) is solely responsible for decisions related to the study (for example, the questions, the methods, the data collection and analysis, and report development). In the past few years, my approach has moved directly into the clients' setting, and I now choose projects where individuals are interested in building their personal and organizational capacity to conduct evaluations on their own after I leave.

4. What is your assessment of the likelihood that you would be able to implement and complete the evaluation as you have described it?

JENNIFER C. GREENE: The likelihood that I could implement and complete this evaluation as proposed is moderate to high, unless I have radically misread the situation or there is vitally important information currently missing from the scenario—for example, a threatened civil rights lawsuit by concerned parents or an educational budget shortfall of millions of dollars in the district. If there are no critical factors missing from the scenario, I feel the likelihood of successful implementation is moderate or high because the design is a relatively modest one, which is intended to fit within the existing rhythms of the school as much as possible and has the potential for generating valuable information for stakeholders in the context.

Challenges to successful implementation are headed by the evaluation design's commitment to including all legitimate stakeholder groups in key evaluation decisions. Evaluators usually believe their work is of considerably more importance than program stakeholders in the context at hand. It remains very difficult and challenging to involve already busy people and people with little history of being invited to participate in the work of evaluation. While this is not a fully participatory evaluation process, it does require meaningful stakeholder involvement in order to be successful. Without such participation, the evaluation risks being an activity disconnected from the lifeblood of teaching and learning in the Bunche–Da Vinci Learning Academy. Yet only with such participation, at least by a handful of influential stakeholders, can the evaluation fulfill its promise.

GARY T. HENRY: Of course, an obstacle to conducting the evaluation would be the amount of funding required, but education evaluation sponsors and policymakers are asking for better evidence before propagating programs of questionable effectiveness. Solid evidence about effectiveness doesn't come cheap, and this evaluation would be expensive. Ideally, an efficacy study, which would have been less costly than the evaluation that I proposed, would have been required before the Da Vinci Learning Model was accepted at Bunche School. It is more common to have policy out in front of evidence than the reverse, unfortunately.

STEWART I. DONALDSON: I have come to appreciate over time that clients, stakeholders, and people in general are highly unpredictable in evaluation practice, especially when you are required to base predictions on superficial information. Programs and organizations like the Bunche Academy and Da Vinci Corporation, are also typically dynamic and unstable. However, if García and Chase are truly interested in professional evaluation and my assumptions are accepted, I think it is very likely that steps 1 and 2 would be implemented with great success. They could be so successful that step 3 is not necessary. If step 3 is needed, I believe it is likely it could be implemented and completed as I have described. But please be cautioned: the devil is almost always in the program or evaluation plan implementation.

JEAN A. KING: Despite the uncertainty, my practice in numerous settings over many years supports two probable results. I am fairly confident that even in the worst-case scenario where the unknowns described above become insurmountable constraints, we could both implement and complete an evaluation process and that it would make at least some difference. First, it would generate new data and compile existing data, enabling us both to attain the proposed evaluation outcomes related to the school's instructional program (that is, knowledge about the implementation of the principal's new system and understanding of the school's parallel test scores) and to make collective sense of what people might do to improve it. Second, the collaborative evaluation process—the active involvement of as many Bunche–Da Vinci faculty and staff as are willing to participate— would likely have its own outcomes. People would pick up the evaluation process by engaging in it, they would unavoidably learn the accountability mandates facing the school, they would develop trust as they reflected together, and, in small ways at first, they would begin to systematize their individual, intuitive evaluation mind-sets.

While I am hopeful that "evaluation present" would generate results for the school, I am less sanguine about "evaluation future": the creation of a viable infrastructure for evaluation at Bunche–Da Vinci. Ideally, at the end of the first year, several components would be in place: the Evaluation Advisory Committee, a subcommittee for studying test scores, a model for highly visible group studies, and perhaps a process for individual action research. But I know how incredibly difficult it is to sustain evaluation activities in schools and other nonprofit organizations. Those who know and support evaluation internally, the key actors to sustain the infrastructure, may leave or become otherwise engaged professionally or personally. External mandates may overwhelm a fledging infrastructure with limited resources. Resources, both those explicit to evaluation (such as data entry and analysis) and those that support it (such as the availability of substitute teachers), may dry up. All of those possibilities are likely at Bunche–Da Vinci. In my experience, though, the school is likely to benefit in the short run from the evaluation activities: people will study the principal's changes, make collective sense of the test scores, and perhaps engage in individual improvements in their classrooms, for example. In addition, as I have recast this evaluation situation, there is the added benefit of building an evaluation infrastructure. The likely beneficiaries of this are some of the individuals who participate—those who increase their evaluation knowledge and skills or the people who gain positive attitudes toward evaluation. Regardless of the outcomes of this study, such individuals may pursue additional training or become leaders of later evaluation efforts.

Editors' Thoughts

Any case scenario, no matter how thoughtfully done, cannot possibly provide all of the information that an evaluator might want to know. It certainly cannot capture all of the nuances of the situation. Theorists were urged to make appropriate assumptions in order to fill in missing information necessary for them to be able to complete the exercise. Explicit statements of understandings and actions within the chapters themselves fail to convey all of the thoughts about the situation that must have run through the minds of each of the chapter writers.

By asking theorists to indicate information that was missing and the major assumptions that they made, we hoped to understand further the mind-set under which they operated. They did not disappoint us. With great clarity, the theorists pointed out a panoply of ideas. Greene expressed dismay about the insufficiency of information about the "educational, organizational, and political context of the school district and its urban setting." Other theorists elaborated on this concern by pointing to such elements as district politics, school attitudes, and "the realities of the community."

The case was complicated by the presence of the Da Vinci Learning Corporation and the need to better understand the organization and its program, as well as further details of the contractual relationship between Da Vinci and the school district.

Assumptions can be only tenuously stated, but even with additional information cannot be affirmed without face-to-face interactions with stakeholders. This characteristic of the exercise, of course, was the basis for much of the difference to be found in presentations. Theorists were allowed (indeed required, because of the lack of information) to make assumptions about the results of interactions. This is perhaps unavoidable in a simulation exercise.

Theorists acknowledged a diversity of theoretical views and prior experience with contexts similar to Bunche–Da Vinci. Greene and King, in particular, were very comfortable with the typicality of the setting in relationship to their experience. Donaldson and Henry were less familiar with this specific kind of setting, but nonetheless felt able to deal with this situation. We do not know whether the theorists would actually behave in practice in the ways described in these chapters. Would Henry, for example, redirect the evaluation question to provide a firm foundation for his approach? Would King either refuse the evaluation or redefine it into a process of long-term, collaborative capacity building, regardless of the client's urgent questions? We only have the stories that each of the authors told and must assume that their evaluation descriptions are a reasonable starting point to what they would do.

Notwithstanding differences in familiarity with setting and necessary assumptions, theorists generally felt comfortable with their ability to propose an evaluation for Bunche–Da Vinci. All of them felt that the product they had produced represented their views on evaluation at an appropriate level. Greene, for one, expressed regrets about elements of the design that she wished that she had had more time to address (mixed methods, internal politics, theory-oriented perspectives). However, even with these minor regrets, she felt that her views had been adequately represented. So too might the other theorists have wished to include additional items in their design.

Evaluators are optimistic about the potential success of their practice. All of the theorists are at least moderately optimistic that they could implement and complete the evaluation as described. The editors of this volume are less sanguine that all would go as proposed. In our view, Greene's evaluation proposal is more typical (in our view) of evaluation practice and moderate in its expectations. We believe that it could be implemented quite adequately, but perhaps without as much stakeholder involvement as she might have wished for. Henry has proposed a very broad-based study that constitutes a multiyear evaluation of the Da Vinci program. It would require a substantial amount of funding and cooperation and participation from many governmental agencies. There could be great difficulties in implementing such an evaluation.

Donaldson proposes an evaluation that focuses heavily on understanding the program theory of the Bunche–Da Vinci model. That aspect of it requires a great deal of participation that might be viewed as helpful but time-consuming. We believe that the step 1 and 2 tasks that he describes are quite doable, and perhaps the rest of the evaluation is as well. King is confident that "even in the worst-case scenario . . . we could both implement and complete the evaluation." We hope that she is right. However, we believe that the amount of time necessary for participating in all of the activities that she describes could be a major impediment. As King notes, she is very selective about the evaluation projects that she is willing to undertake and engages in a process of reconnoitering and doing substantial upfront work in order to determine whether to accept the assignment. By engaging in the process, she has been forced to make the assumption that Bunche–Da Vinci passes the test. But her response to the first question casts some doubt on whether that assumption is correct.

References

Donaldson, S. I., and Gooler, L. E. "Theory-Driven Evaluation in Action: Lessons from a $20 Million Statewide Work and Health Initiative." *Evaluation and Program Planning,* 2003, *26,* 355–366.

Donaldson, S. I., Graham, J. W., and Hansen, W. B. "Testing the Generalizability of Intervening Mechanism Theories: Understanding the Effects of School-Based Substance Use Prevention Interventions." *Journal of Behavioral Medicine,* 1994, *17,* 195–216.

Donaldson, S. I., Graham, J. W., Piccinin, A. M., and Hansen, W. B. "Resistance-Skills Training and Onset of Alcohol Use: Evidence for Beneficial and Potentially Harmful Effects in Public Schools and in Private Catholic Schools." *Health Psychology,* 1995, *14,* 291–300.

Fitzpatrick, J. "Dialog with Stewart Donaldson." *American Journal of Evaluation,* 2002, *23*(3), 347–365.

Lipsey, M. W., and Wilson, D. B. "The Efficacy of Psychological, Educational, and Behavioral Treatment: Confirmation from Meta-Analysis." *American Psychologist,* 1993, *48,* 1181–1209.

MARVIN C. ALKIN *is an emeritus professor in the Social Research Methodology Division in the Graduate School of Education and Information Studies at University of California, Los Angeles.*

CHRISTINA A. CHRISTIE *is an assistant professor and associate director of the Institute of Organizational and Program Evaluation Research at Claremont Graduate University.*

JENNIFER C. GREENE *is a professor of educational psychology at the University of Illinois, Urbana-Champaign.*

GARY T. HENRY *is a professor in the Andrew Young School of Policy Studies and Department of Political Science at Georgia State University.*

STEWART I. DONALDSON *is dean and professor of psychology at the School of Behavioral and Organizational Sciences, Claremont Graduate University.*

JEAN A. KING *is a professor at the University of Minnesota, where she coordinates the Evaluation Studies Program in the Department of Educational Policy and Administration.*

8

*The volume editors provide a comparative analysis of the
evaluation approaches employed by each of the theorists
relative to a number of important evaluation issues.*

Unraveling Theorists' Evaluation Reality

Marvin C. Alkin, Christina A. Christie

The theorists in this volume have confronted the exercise presented to them
in vastly different ways. As editors, we asked them "to consider how you
would evaluate this program" and "to make and specify assumptions about
the program context." The primary task, however, was to describe "a course
of action, which may have consequences that lead to other evaluation design
decisions." All of the theorists did indeed do this. There was great diversity
in the evaluation approaches presented and, of course, in the presentation
of approaches. As mentioned in Chapter Two, we anticipated diversity on
both of these dimensions and were pleased to see that it emerged. Otherwise
our experimental exercise would have been, dare we say, uninteresting. In
this chapter, we explore the differences in approaches that are evident to us,
as well as the similarities (which ought to be just as remarkable in some
instances) on several dimensions of evaluation practice. We will comment
first, however, on each theorist's overall approach to the task before moving on to the discussion of comparing approaches, and have included a
visual summary at the end of the chapter in Table 8.1.

Tackling the Exercise: Overall Format and Approach

Each of the four theorists presented his or her evaluation proposal creatively—describing to the reader what it would be like to walk through an
evaluation "in his or her shoes." What would we encounter, and how would
we deal with it? Henry's approach was relatively straightforward. He made
specific assumptions about what stakeholders wanted out of the evaluation
and then proceeded to establish a design. Greene and King discussed at

New Directions for Evaluation, no. 106, Summer 2005 © Wiley Periodicals, Inc.

length the kinds of interactions that would take place and processes to be implemented, which would lead to further evaluation activities. And Donaldson engaged the reader as an interviewee for a position on his evaluation team. This mixture of format is what we had hoped for. We believe that the way theorists chose to portray their approach to evaluation, in fact, provides insights into their way of thinking about and approaching evaluation.

Theorists' Assumptions and General Evaluation Process

The case scenario in Chapter One was designed to provide answers to many of the potential questions an evaluator may have about the program but obviously left many unanswered questions. The absence of interaction with real-life stakeholders required that each theorist make assumptions, both implicit and explicit, about the case: its stakeholders, context, resources, and the like. In general, theorists made assumptions that moved the evaluation along in a direction that would accommodate the theorists' proclivities. Availability of resources for the evaluation serves as a good example of the kinds of key assumptions made.

Theorists made pivotal assumptions about both the financial and human resources available for the conduct of their evaluation. Henry, for example, assumes that resources will be secured to conduct a multisite evaluation of the program model. Donaldson, in contrast, explicitly states that he assumed that resources were limited and designed his evaluation accordingly, even commenting that if resources were assumed to be unlimited, he would have designed the evaluation differently. Greene also created a design mindful of monetary restrictions. King does not assume that limitless financial resources are available; however, she does make the assumption that stakeholders will be highly committed to and involved in the evaluation. This assumption necessitates a significant human resource commitment.

Obviously, the theorists' assumptions went beyond what financial resources are available. Many assumptions were also made about which stakeholders will be contacted, stakeholders' responses to theorists' proposals about actions to be taken, and, in some instances, the consequences of those actions. Our analysis of each theorist's approach will bring to bear some of the other more important assumptions made.

Theorists' Approaches

In this section, we first summarize the evaluation designs presented by each theorist, pointing to some of the unique aspects of that theorist's presentation. Following this discussion, we present the particular themes that emerged to us across theorists' designs. In some instances, these themes highlight commonalities in presentations. Conversely, a theme may be developed to distinguish theorists' presentations.

Jennifer C. Greene. Greene proposed a "value-engaged approach." She noted that this approach is derived from Stake's concern for responsiveness, but is supplemented with values engagement drawn from democratic and culturally responsive traditions in evaluation. In her chapter, we note the familiar features of evaluation that are present. First, she attempts to develop an understanding of the context and the program to be evaluated. She then works with a variety of stakeholders to identify key evaluation questions and sets up a procedure for establishing criteria for making judgments of program quality. Next, Greene established an evaluation design that incorporated multiple and mixed methods for acquiring information and attended to the process of conducting the evaluation in ways that influenced an evolving evaluation design. Greene did not comment specifically on evaluation reporting, but presumably it would involve a combination of written reports and "meaningful dialogues with stakeholders." Finally, she proposed conducting a meta-evaluation. One of our colleagues, Lynn Winters, assistant superintendent for planning and evaluation in the Long Beach (California) Unified School District, on reading the chapter, suggested that the approach reminds her of many evaluations that she has seen: "I would like to know what this [value-engaged] approach really means in terms of perspective and how it affects methodology and the kinds of questions one would ask."

We acknowledge Winters's point. Nevertheless, the attention to broad-based stakeholders, while it might be common in many approaches, is substantially more intensive in what Greene proposes. Indeed, the evaluation priorities emerged from discussions with parent communities as well as from a discussion at a faculty meeting. Moreover, the criteria for making judgments of program quality were established through discussions with diverse stakeholders. As noted in one of Greene's memos, initial specification of criteria for making judgments emerged not only from the school community, but also from parents and families. It is perhaps difficult to envisage in a written evaluation design the sensitivity of the evaluator to principles of social justice that undergird each activity.

And so we raise the issue about how possible it is to judge differences in theoretical applications by the written document that is produced. To a large extent, it is necessary to observe Greene as she engages in the evaluation, who she listens to, what special efforts she puts forth, and so forth.

Gary T. Henry. Henry's approach is concerned with identifying the mechanisms that lead to program outcomes. He focuses on the efficacy of the overall Da Vinci program model, and the evaluation he proposes is designed to do just that. There are no surprises in his design. He offers a well-thought-out quasi-experimental study. In order to conduct this study, Henry assumed that resources could be secured to support this large-scale design, which includes twenty-five Da Vinci model schools and twenty-five comparison schools. Although he does not detail the budget for his study, he does suggest offering each comparison school $10,000 for participation (totaling $250,000). And so it is important to note that Henry's design would likely far exceed the cost of implementing any of the other theorists' designs.

Henry convenes an evaluation advisory group consisting of representatives from the evaluation funder, the state educational office, the state superintendent's office, and other high-level organizations to advise the evaluation and aid in the interpretations of findings. It is apparent from the selection of advisory board members that Henry's evaluation is not driven at the local school level. He does, however, suggest including local school stakeholders to identify the values of those affected by the program, and uses sampling techniques to ensure representation at levels. At the initial stage of the evaluation, which he refers to as values inquiry, he offers both qualitative and quantitative methods for identifying stakeholders' most highly valued program outcomes. He then develops a program theory, with the assistance of the Da Vinci program developers and teachers systematically selected from four schools, that focuses on the outcomes identified during the values inquiry stage. Outcomes are measured by extant achievement measures, and program implementation is measured using multiple data sources. Henry is the only theorist to describe in detail the sampling methods and data analysis techniques that he would use. This is seemingly because Henry's approach relies heavily on the success of the implementation of the study design and data collection procedures.

Henry was the only theorist to state that one of the explicit purposes of the evaluation was to assess the merit and worth of the program. Winters points out that the strength of Henry's chapter is that he was "proactive about focusing the evaluation on the Da Vinci Model. . . . He saw through . . . to the 'core beast' needing review . . . [for] useful policy decisions." We recognize the concern about the evaluation of the Bunche–Da Vinci model but would like to note that by moving in that direction, Henry bypasses the immediate concern for satisfying local concerns. His concern for generating information for policy decisions for the State of Columbia is, however, what differentiates the focus of his evaluation and, subsequently, his evaluation approach.

Stewart I. Donaldson. Donaldson's application of program theory–driven evaluation science as it is described in his chapter has three steps: (1) develop a program theory, (2) identify evaluation questions, and (3) design and conduct the evaluation. Donaldson tells us that the first two steps should take about three months and that he would contract for steps 1 and 2 before contracting to conduct step 3.

Overall, Donaldson describes his role as one of a facilitator of discussion. He first facilitates a discussion among stakeholders to establish a program theory. Donaldson described this as an interactive process of making stakeholders' assumptions and understandings of the program explicit— that is, they develop a program theory. He does not describe for us the specific group of stakeholders that would participate in this process. Nevertheless, he assumes that at Bunche–Da Vinci, the program theory is anchored in student performance—even though he anticipates that some stakeholders may object to this. The plausibility of the program theory is then assessed using extant literature and revised accordingly. Evaluation questions are formulated that would focus on curriculum implementation, program operations and educational service delivery, and program outcomes. Although stakeholders' opinions about the value of each question are considered, it seems that Donaldson, while cognizant of the program theory, makes the final decision about which questions to pursue.

In Donaldson's evaluation, methodological choices are informed by the program theory. He speaks of the evaluator as a facilitator of a process in which the evaluator educates stakeholders about the benefits and challenges of using particular methods and leads to agreement about which data sources and collection techniques will be used. He also stresses the importance of establishing criteria of merit with stakeholders to justify conclusions and recommendations and to increase use.

Shadish, Cook, and Leviton (1991) describe theory-driven evaluation (some say too generously) as a comprehensive "third-generation" approach to evaluation, one that incorporates methods from previous evaluation theories. When reading Donaldson's chapter, one cannot help but detect methods from other theoretical approaches. For example, his attention to García and Chase, the program administrators, reminds us of the work of user-oriented evaluation theorists who express concern for developing evaluations attentive to the needs of decision makers. Donaldson offers the Program Evaluation Standards as a means for establishing and checking evaluation processes. There is also direct reference to establishing criteria of merit, a process that Scriven argues is an essential component of any evaluation. Of course, there is the focus on establishing the connection between program outcomes and processes, which Campbell and Cook argue is the purpose of evaluation. Finally, Donaldson describes the evaluator as a facilitator of stakeholder beliefs and values, reminiscent of democratic approaches. Thus, Donaldson's approach could be seen as an eclectic mix of procedures and processes, formulated around a program theory.

Jean A. King. King's chapter is particularly significant in the way in which it demonstrates the thinking process of an evaluator. In King's case, we have an evaluator who, as a consequence of being concerned with evaluation utilization, is focused on building evaluation capacity as an end result of the evaluation process. And how is capacity built? At its core, capacity building involves the creation of structures for attaining the active involvement of school-based participants. This means that active learning (about evaluation) must take place: committees are engaged in deciding what is to be done (an advisory group). King structures activities to build an evaluation infrastructure. This is done through systematically seeking to understand the context. Various direct activities to enhance infrastructure are proposed, including having staff participate in a small-scale, but nevertheless visible, participatory inquiry project.

But in discussing the activities proposed by King, we clearly have put the cart before the horse. King proposes a great deal of upfront work before she even agrees to do the evaluation. She engages in a self-evaluation to determine whether the evaluation situation is a good fit for her own skills, interests, and background, and then some "reconnoitering" and informal research are required. She wants to know about the specific context and to some extent about comparable programs. All of this precedes the negotiation of the contract, in which she sets specific conditions to be fulfilled before agreeing to participate.

One of the conditions that King mandates is a substantial (perhaps very substantial) amount of active involvement by school personnel. We wonder about the prevalence of situations where such involvement is possible. Does insistence on active involvement mean that a school like Bunche–Da Vinci would not obtain King's services, and she would do evaluations only in settings where teachers are not so overwhelmed?

Building evaluation capacity takes time. This is quite evident in King's description of the evaluation process. It is indeed worthwhile and rewarding to not only provide information on the success of a program, but also to create a structure in which people respect and relish evaluation information and continually engage in the process as a means of improving their program. Building an evaluation community is hard work. Do the parties involved in Bunche–Da Vinci have the patience to wait for the answers they seek? Perhaps many evaluation situations are not instances for potential evaluation capacity building.

King addresses some of these issues in Chapter Seven. She expresses optimism about the potential for completing the evaluation. We wondered, however, whether there are lost opportunities, that is, evaluations in which she chose not to participate. Does her stance reflect the autonomy of a university-based evaluator and not that of an evaluator in full-time practice? She, like us, has the luxury of deciding what evaluation studies she would do in addition to her university employment. Are there some markers that she uses at the outset of the project that will allow her to make early decisions as to whether this is an evaluation in which she could or should be involved?

Common Themes

Of interest to us was the extent to which theorists' approaches were similar. For example, some of the steps that Greene and King proposed with respect to engaging stakeholders are particularly comparable. However, the intent behind the action, as described by the theorist, is different. Acknowledging this, we engaged in a lengthy discussion about the extent to which a theorist's intention behind an action is, or is not, evident in the action itself. Let us explain further.

We understand that the intent that motivated Greene and King to engage stakeholders was different because they told us so. We asked them to explain what they would do and why—and they did. King wanted to build evaluation capacity by engaging stakeholders in the process of conducting the evaluation. Greene wanted to engage a broad spectrum of stakeholders in the evaluation process in order to be responsive to their values. In our view, there was a difference in intensity in the engagement of stakeholders. Perhaps King's approach involved more "doing" and Greene's more thinking, judging, and communicating. But in any case, imagine being a stakeholder who is unfamiliar and unconcerned with evaluation terminology or theoretical nuance. The action, absent a description of what it is intended to yield, looks much the same. So we ask the question, When similar actions or practices are motivated by different intents, that is, if King and Greene engage stakeholders in a similar fashion but do so to accomplish a different end, how can one be guaranteed that King's action produced what was intended—and indeed not what Greene intended it to produce instead? This observation may help to explain why in Christie's study (2003) of evaluation theorists' practice, some theorists with seemingly different theoretical approaches, when asked to describe only their practices (absent an explanation of intent or motivation), quantitatively look similar.

On Theory. Each theorist was very consistent with his or her own purported theoretical position—perhaps too much so. Again, the process of being selected to write a chapter may have led the theorists to believe that they were commissioned to portray how an evaluation would be conducted from the vantage point of their specific theoretical position. Indeed, each of the chapter authors commented on his or her perspective on evaluation as a part of the evaluation proposal. Perhaps this is not surprising. The orientation of an evaluator sets the context for what an evaluator proposes and how he or she will do it. Thus, we find little to comment on with respect to adherence to theoretical position. To the extent to which the context matched his or her own theoretical position, each theorist proposed an evaluation along the lines of that position.

While the theorists chosen for participation in this exercise represented each of the branches of our evaluation theory tree (Greene, values; King, use; and Donaldson and Henry, methods), they are not, and could not be, representative, in any sense, of all theorists who might be depicted on the branch of the tree on which they have been placed. We view Greene as a "democratic evaluator." Yet there are differences between her approach and, say, those of Stake (2003) or House (House and Howe, 1999). We see the extent of her desire for substantive inclusion of underrepresented individuals in all stages of the evaluation as greater than that of Stake. Furthermore, we believe that the extent to which her inclusion principles would extend to advocating for groups in the absence of broad participation would be less than that which House (2003) might employ. Obviously there are vast differences in the way that she conceives of evaluation from what Scriven (also concerned about valuing) would propose (2004). To give one further example, King and others (for example, Cousins and Whitmore, 1998; Preskill and Torres, 1999) on the upper reaches of the use branch who are strongly engaged in evaluation capacity building differ from other use-oriented evaluators such as Stufflebeam (2003) and even Patton (1997). (We cannot help but note also that on the face of it, there are similarities that go across branches. One theorist can generally agree with another's procedures and actions, but the intentions behind the actions are the basis for theoretical nuances that make a difference.) Thus, we are not attempting to demonstrate differences in evaluation practice between broad theoretical perspectives. Rather, this volume describes four theorists' unique perspectives and how, from that perspective, they would engage in the conduct of an evaluation, given the particular context of the case scenario presented.

Stakeholder Engagement. Each of the theorists in this volume addresses the need for stakeholder involvement. Indeed, by now, this has become an implicit part of almost all evaluation theories (Christie, 2003). Yet there are substantial differences between theorists in the choice of stakeholders to be included, the stages at which they participate, and the nature of their involvement. King's stakeholders are primarily Bunche–Da Vinci faculty and staff. While others' inputs are reflected in the process, the focus in evaluation capacity building for King is the primary users, primarily staff and teachers. These users are engaged as primary "doers" at every stage of the evaluation. They are not simply consulted to provide input, and they are not stakeholders in the sense of having their views reflected and advocated by the evaluator. Instead, their stakeholder role is active engagement in all phases of the evaluation.

Greene also engages stakeholders substantially at most phases of the evaluation. Her stakeholder group is broad based, with particular attention to the inclusion of people traditionally underrepresented or, in the absence of sufficient participation, to the reflection of their views.

Donaldson engages only García and Chase in his discussion of the evaluation, although he talks specifically about having them identify leaders of key stakeholder groups for him to contact to describe the evaluation plan. There is no discussion, however, of the role of these additional stakeholders in the evaluation process. Beyond Chase and García, we never learn who these stakeholders are in the case of Bunche–Da Vinci or exactly how their roles are envisioned.

Henry is concerned with having broad stakeholder input, particularly at the values inquiry stage of his evaluation. Broad-based stakeholder participation, however, is not maintained throughout the evaluation process. In fact, it seems to taper as Henry moves through his evaluation plan. That is, the most significant level of stakeholder participation occurs at the beginning stages, including program theory development, but interpretation of findings is left to the evaluator and the evaluation advisory committee. Of course, this advisory committee comprises individuals with a vested interest in the program, but they represent just a small segment of possible stakeholder groups.

Use. Use has become a central theme in the evaluation theory literature. There is general agreement that information yielded from evaluations is intended to be used. There is debate, however, about the extent to which potential evaluation use should serve as a driving force behind an evaluation's design and implementation. Nonetheless, most theorists suggest that evaluators include stakeholders in the evaluation process in order to increase the odds that the evaluation will be used.

Thinking about stakeholder involvement in the evaluation process as a means for increasing use, we distinguish between depth and breadth of involvement (House, 2003). When referring to depth of involvement, we are considering the extent to which stakeholders participate in the process; when referring to breadth, we are considering the number of stakeholders and constituencies reached during the evaluation process. In our experience, often one is sacrificed at the expense of the other. That is, it is very difficult to have both great depth and breadth of stakeholder participation in the evaluation process, and, as a result, the evaluator often has to choose between the two. This choice, however, is often determined from the outset by the overall evaluation approach.

The theorists in this volume, by and large, did not address specifically what they would do with respect to use. It is our belief that the task presented to the theorists (to describe how they would study a particular program) did not lend itself to an in-depth discussion about use. And so we surmise that this is a function of the task rather than a conscious decision on the part of theorists to not attend to the topic in depth. Thus, we will address use as it related to stakeholder involvement in the evaluation process.

King addressed use most explicitly, which is what one would presume based on the nature of her approach. She is entirely focused on use, but not primarily the use of specific evaluation findings. Rather, her concern is with what is referred to in the literature as process use (Patton, 1997). Focusing on the small group of stakeholders within the school, she seeks to engage them in the process of evaluation to build organizational capacity. Her approach involves deep stakeholder involvement.

Greene's approach involves somewhat less depth of stakeholder involvement but considerably greater breadth. The extensive inclusion of a wide range of stakeholders, while not focusing specifically on use, presumes that a higher quality of use will occur—one that reflects values of social justice.

Relative to the other theorists, Henry proposes to involve the largest number of stakeholders. As such, he is concerned with breadth of stakeholder involvement and broad use of his findings. Use of information at the local level is important, but is offset by a value for generating information to be used to inform policy decisions. Donaldson involves stakeholders at the local level, but also mentions involving stakeholders beyond those identified in the case. Although not stated explicitly, we presume that Donaldson is concerned with use beyond the program level, for example, is interested in generating information for the Da Vinci Learning Corporation and the school district, but is less concerned in this particular evaluation context with providing for state policy decisions (like Henry).

Program Theory. All the theorists in this volume acknowledge the importance of understanding program theory as part of the evaluation. However, the emphasis placed on the role of program theory in the evaluation process is vastly different. This is not surprising given each theorist's primary focus.

Greene is mainly concerned about value-engaged evaluation; her focus is primarily on the inclusion of the values and interests of underrepresented groups. Henry expresses concern for performing evaluation in policy contexts—which usually requires the use of experimental or quasi-experimental designs to be considered appropriately valid. Thus, program theory is important but secondary to design concerns. King, in her attention to building evaluation capacity, is more concerned with the individuals and the process in which they engage. Clearly Donaldson's primary focus is program theory as the route for understanding the relationship between and impact of program activities.

The cornerstone of Donaldson's approach is the development of a program theory. Once developed, the program theory prescribes and orders the questions that the evaluation will address. The evaluation is then built around the questions yielded from an analysis of the program theory. Winters notes that "Donaldson convinces me 'assumption-examining' is an important step in the evaluation design and is a perspective that doesn't show up explicitly anywhere else but drives all of the activities in other chapters." Indeed, Greene and Henry in particular acknowledge the necessity of understanding a program's theory. Donaldson's approach, however, moves beyond just understanding a program theory by defining program goals and testing the relationship of proposed activities to those goals.

Henry uses the program theory as a means for determining the connections between program processes and outcomes. He is most concerned, however, with examining program outcomes, and so it is not necessary to connect each program outcome to a program process. Different from Donaldson, Henry identifies the primary questions for the evaluation prior to program theory development. The program theory is used to help the evaluator determine where to look when explaining program outcomes.

Program theory is not the focal point of Greene's approach to evaluation. Yet a concern for "understanding the conceptual rationales" of the Bunche–Da Vinci is a part of her approach. Her strong attempt at understanding the school context adds light to her consideration of the program's theory.

While program theory is not central to the work of King, she nonetheless acknowledges its importance in some of the activities in which evaluation participants engage. For example, in her chapter discussion related to making sense of test scores, she notes that the committee engaged in this activity "might develop program theory that would plan backward from the necessary achievement outcomes to identify explicit strategies to increase learning in specific areas."

Social Justice. We would argue that most professionals conducting evaluations of social and educational programs think of themselves as service providers and hope to be promoting justice, equity, and social betterment through their work (Donaldson and Christie, forthcoming). Some evaluators, however, pursue this (lofty) goal more intentionally through their actions. These approaches are sometimes described as social justice approaches. Christie (2003) found that those concerned with intentionally promoting social justice through their evaluation actions can be differentiated. From one perspective, the evaluator intends to promote social justice by increasing representation (House, 1993). From another perspective, social justice can be promoted by empowering those involved with the evaluation (Fetterman, 1996). Social justice approaches to evaluation are distinguished, however, from other approaches that pursue social betterment. All of the theorists in the volume expressed or implied a general concern for promoting social betterment. All were highly motivated by the desire to provide information that would improve the education of students. There are differences, however, in the ways in which this concern is addressed throughout the evaluation process and the extent of emphasis on social justice.

The title of Henry's chapter, "In Pursuit of Social Betterment," reflects his concern for conducting evaluations that contribute to the social good. He does not, however, intend to conduct a social justice evaluation as described by House or Fetterman, although his proposal to involve a broad group of stakeholders and the methods proposed for doing so (sampling, surveying, and focus groups) reflect, at least in part, some of the ideas put forth by House (for example, in House, 2003). Donaldson indicates a desire to implement a place that could "help them improve the way they educate students" (again, social betterment, but not particularly social justice). King also is clearly focused on social betterment rather than social justice as an agenda. She, like the others above, is implicitly concerned about issues related to social justice. However, her focus is social betterment—specifically through building the evaluation capacity of the school. Greene undoubtedly has the strongest social justice agenda in her design. She follows a value-engaged approach, which aspires to meet the educational needs of people traditionally underrepresented: racial and ethnic minorities, low-income people, and others.

Methods. All of the theorists proposed a mixed-method approach to studying Bunche–Da Vinci. Some were more specific about which methods they would use and when. Henry, for example, proposed using focus groups to identify the stakeholder values during the values identification phase of his evaluation. He said that he would later use observation methods to study program implementation. Nevertheless, the data collection methods used to study program outcomes are primarily quantitative. As mentioned previously, Henry is the only theorist who described a specific data analysis plan. This description provides a rationale for the data collected as well as an understanding of how program success will be determined.

We found it interesting that both Henry and Donaldson stated explicitly that their approaches are "method neutral." And this may be because their particular approaches are at times characterized as being primarily quantitative. This in fact was the case in the evaluation designs proposed in this volume. Nevertheless, it may be important for both Henry and Donaldson to state that their methodological choices are not determined a priori and that they are not limited to quantitative methods. But as evidenced by the proposals offered to evaluate Bunche–Da Vinci, each of their approaches stresses the importance of measuring program impact in a way that lends itself to the use of quantitative measures. In fact, it is our opinion that neither Henry nor Donaldson would consider examining Bunche–Da Vinci's program outcomes or impacts qualitatively, that is, to simply describe a program outcome, without some statistical evidence of its impact. Both, however, propose using qualitative methods to measure program fidelity and implementation.

Greene's design has some quantitative methodological components, primarily related to outcome measures, but it rests most heavily on qualitative methods. There is a strong focus in her evaluation work on discussions, conversations, classroom and school observations, and interviews with both staff and parents.

King's methodology can perhaps be best described as participatory engagement designed to obtain skills and build capacity. There is some quantitative analysis (engaged in by program participants conducting a mini study). However, the methodology of qualitative approaches dominates the design.

Table 8.1 presents a comparison of the theory chapters in terms of the dimensions discussed in this chapter.

Last Word

We view the theorists' chapters in this volume as a set of case examples. Thus, our interpretation of these cases is subject to validation of some type. As Yin (1989) notes, "A major way of improving the quality of case studies . . . is to have the draft cases reviewed by those who have been the subject of the study" (p. 144). We therefore invited the authors to provide their "last words" on the topic; most accepted the invitation.

JENNIFER C. GREENE: Evaluation is a complex social practice with multiple, interwoven strands. One strand represents the technical aspects of our

Table 8.1. A Comparison of Approaches

	Approach	Stakeholders	Stakeholders: Depth of Participation	Use Concern	Program Theory	Social Justice	Methods
Greene	Value engaged	Broad based, attention to inclusion of traditionally underrepresented people	Very substantial engagement at most phases	Use reflects values of social justice	As an aid in understanding the conceptual rationales of the program	Social justice	Mixed methods—heavily qualitative
Henry	Quasi-experimental	Broad stakeholder input	Moderate participation at beginning stages	Information used to inform policy decisions	As an aid in understanding cause-and-effect relationships	Social betterment	Primarily quantitative
Donaldson	Program theory evaluation science	Program management	Engagement primarily at early stages	Primarily used at the program level	Route for understanding relationship between and impact of program activities	Social betterment	Primarily quantitative
King	Building evaluation capacity	Primary users: staff and teachers	Active engagement in all phases	Process use	As an aid to stakeholder planning	Social betterment	Mixed methods—primarily qualitative

work. To be good evaluation technicians, we use our expertise in social inquiry methodology. The ways in which we craft an evaluation design, select methods and samples, analyze and interpret data, and fashion evaluation reports all represent the quality of our technical knowledge. The evaluations presented in this volume well represent this technical dimension of our work, even as they offer varied perspectives on it. Another strand of evaluation practice is substantive and contextual. We endeavor to understand the quality of a given human endeavor in the specific form it takes in the particular contexts being evaluated. This strand of our work requires some conceptual and experiential familiarity with the evaluand and the contexts at hand. In this volume, the substance of relevance is schoolwide educational reform as packaged by the Da Vinci Learning Corporation *and* as implemented in a particular underresourced urban context. The editors of the volume appropriately noted that the four evaluators have differential conceptual and experiential familiarity with schoolwide educational reform in underresourced public school settings, as this indeed matters to the quality and influence of our work.

A third strand of evaluation practice is sociopolitical. It concerns the positioning of evaluation with respect to the program and policies being evaluated and relates directly to intended evaluation purposes and audiences. This strand is among the most contested in evaluation, as it invokes the multiple interests of diverse stakeholders, all of which are legitimate but some of which can be competing, even conflicting. The different evaluations presented in this volume clearly differ in terms of whose interests are addressed and which stakeholder concerns are privileged.

A final strand of evaluation practice is relational. It pertains to the evaluator's presence in the context being evaluated, to the roles and identities she takes on, to her interactions and communications with others in that context. In many ways, the other strands of evaluation are enacted through such roles, communications, and relationships; thus, the relational strand is a powerful one. I endeavored to share the relational strands of my envisioned evaluation in the Bunche–Da Vinci context through memos that referred to evaluative gatherings and events *and* that conveyed particular norms, notably of respect and reciprocity. Yet I fully appreciate the editors' perceptive insight that a linear written text cannot really capture this relational strand of evaluation, as it takes meaningful form only in action.

STEWART I. DONALDSON: Why have Alkin and Christie passed up the golden opportunity to do what this volume is all about: evaluate? As they pointed out, Shadish, Cook, and Leviton (1991) evaluated the various theories of evaluation practice they critically examined, and theory-driven evaluation emerged in a very favorable light. I was secretly hoping to find my plan for evaluating Bunche–Da Vinci to be ranked number 1 out of 4, and dreading the possibility, and ready to counter (or employ ego defense mechanisms), if it was ranked anything less. If they do not want to evaluate us themselves, how about submitting these plans to a panel of experts, principals, teachers, or parents for judgment?

I suggest summative evaluation jokingly in my last word, where it is safe (I think) to assume they will not get any ideas along these lines, to help underscore the point that this exercise was not about which plan is the best. In fact, I think the answer to the questions above is that this exercise and volume is not about evaluating merit, but rather a good example of creative, descriptive research on evaluation theory and practice. Alkin and Christie's collegial approach to this exercise and research on evaluation theory and practice more generally (for example, Alkin and Christie, 2004; Christie, 2003) is refreshing, exemplary, and sorely needed. In my evaluation, these works make significant contributions toward advancing our understanding of the emerging discipline and profession of evaluation.

But let me end by evaluating a few of their observations about my plan for helping Bunche–Da Vinci. The discrepancies noted below may be due more to the lack of detail in my chapter, or my ability to communicate well in this format, than to errors of analysis. First, I give them an A for describing my approach as "an eclectic mix of procedures and processes, formulated around a program theory." Engaging diverse stakeholders in an effort to fully understand their program (the evaluand), and then using that shared understanding to present evaluation options based on the best procedures, process, and methods available today (from across approaches and theories of practice) sums up my approach well. In contrast, Alkin and Christie's observations about stakeholder involvement and that the evaluation team would determine the evaluation questions made me realize I did not state clearly enough that I would engage as many stakeholders as made sense in the light of human resource and financial constraints and that the evaluation clients (stakeholder representatives), not the evaluation team, would ultimately decide which questions to pursue.

I was intrigued that both Gary T. Henry and I used the "method-neutral" defense, and by the bold statement that we would not consider qualitative methods for assessing Bunche–Da Vinci's program outcomes or impacts. Although I know there is something to this in terms of our training and background, I would not like to think that my team would shy away from qualitative work here if the clients (stakeholders) decided this was the best option. I must add, though, that the case description seems to suggest to me that test scores and quantitative measures of outcomes are important to at least some of the key stakeholders.

Finally, there has been much discussion in recent years about improving the cost-benefit and cost-effectiveness analysis of programs under evaluation. Now that I have spent some time on the other side of the fence (developing and managing programs), I am more acutely aware that we need to apply cost-benefit and cost-effectiveness concepts more routinely to our evaluation plans as well. So in the end, not only did I assume there might be human resource and financial constraints in this case, I strived to develop a plan that would allow the stakeholders to prevent risks involved with commissioning external evaluations and would help them manage the costs of investing in this type of professional service.

JEAN A. KING: For me the Bunche–Da Vinci scenario raises the definitional specter that continues to haunt our field: exactly what activities the portmanteau concept of program evaluation envelopes. Baizerman and others (2002) state that evaluation capacity building (ECB) is its own form of practice, distinct from evaluation. Reading this chapter's analysis, I tend to agree. ECB will not work in many settings, and if it is done poorly, it may reinforce participants' negative attitudes toward evaluation—hence, the importance of situational analysis and detailed preparation prior to launching a project. To my mind, it is better not to take a contract than to proceed and fail.

This leads me to a more general point: I want to make clear that my evaluation practice includes more than ECB projects. Because I work primarily with organizations that have little money for evaluation—school districts and nonprofit organizations—my experience over time has led me to participatory methods and capacity building, first because staff members can make time for a process they believe is valuable and, second, because, by building internal capacity, the evaluation process may survive longer than a single funded project.

Students in the courses I teach quickly learn that the best answer to many procedural questions in evaluation is, "It depends," because it usually does. Alkin and Christie rightly note that a key challenge in responding to this scenario (in contrast to an actual situation) is that we were forced to make assumptions in the absence of real information regarding the "it depends" decisions. The assumptions I made stem from my capacity-building experiences in three organizations: an urban high school with an array of social and instructional problems, a large school district with constraining resources and diversity issues, and a long-time social service agency facing major changes in staff and clientele. My experience validates the opposite of what Alkin and Christie suggest: that active involvement by personnel in the Bunche–Da Vinci case or in similar situations is unlikely.

On the contrary, in seemingly desperate situations—but with the right leadership and commitment—program evaluation can become a mechanism for addressing what may seem to be the overwhelming nature of the context. Rather than adding one more item to a long to-do list, it can generate information that allows staff to tackle critical areas of practice, quickly harvest so-called low-hanging fruit, and develop strategies for long-term improvement. They can generate visible evidence that hope lives in this setting—that people can actively do something to change the circumstances both in which they work and in their clients' lives. Is this easy to do? Of course not. The phrase "with the right leadership and commitment" points to at least two variables that, in my experience, are a necessary condition for success, one or both of which unfortunately are often lacking in such settings. My commitment is to identify places where the process may work long term, hoping in so doing to sustain long-term improvements in the organization and in the lives of children and participants.

References

Alkin, M., and Christie, C. "An Evaluation Theory Tree." In M. Alkin, *Evaluation Roots: Tracing Theorists' Views and Influences.* Thousand Oaks, Calif.: Sage, 2004.

Baizerman, M., Compton, D. W., and Stockdill, S. H. "New Directions for ECB." In D. W. Compton, M. Baizerman, and S. H. Stockdill (eds.), *The Art, Craft, and Science of Evaluation Capacity Building.* New Directions for Evaluation, no. 93. San Francisco: Jossey-Bass, 2002.

Christie, C. A. "What Guides Evaluation? A Study of How Evaluation Practice Maps onto Evaluation Theory." In C. A. Christie (ed.), *The Practice-Theory Relationship in Evaluation.* New Directions for Evaluation, no. 97. San Francisco: Jossey-Bass, 2003.

Cousins, J. B., and Whitmore, E. "Framing Participatory Evaluation." In E. Whitmore (ed.), *Understanding and Practicing Participatory Evaluation.* New Directions in Evaluation, no. 80. San Francisco: Jossey-Bass, 1998.

Donaldson, S. I., and Christie, C. A. "The 2004 Claremont Debate: Lipsey vs. Scriven. Determining Causality in Program Evaluation and Applied Research: Should Experimental Evidence Be the Gold Standard?" *Journal of Multidisciplinary Evaluation,* forthcoming.

Fetterman, D. M. "Empowerment Evaluation: An Introduction to Theory and Practice." In D. M. Fetterman, S. J. Kartarian, and A. Wandersman (eds.), *Empowerment Evaluation.* Thousand Oaks, Calif.: Sage, 1996.

House, E. R. *Professional Evaluation: Social Impact and Political Consequences.* Thousand Oaks, Calif.: Sage, 1993.

House, E. R. "Stakeholder Bias." In C. A. Christie (ed.), *The Practice-Theory Relationship in Evaluation.* New Directions for Evaluation, no. 97. San Francisco: Jossey-Bass, 2003.

House, E. R., and Howe, K. R. *Values in Evaluation and Social Research.* Thousand Oaks, Calif.: Sage, 1999.

Patton, M. Q. *Utilization-Focused Evaluation.* (3rd ed.) Thousand Oaks, Calif.: Sage, 1997.

Preskill, H., and Torres, R. T. *Evaluative Inquiry for Learning in Organizations.* Thousand Oaks, Calif.: Sage, 1999.

Scriven, M. "Reflections." In M. Alkin (ed.), *Evaluation Roots: Tracing Theorists' Views and Influences.* Thousand Oaks, Calif.: Sage, 2004.

Shadish, W., Cook, T. and Leviton, L. *Foundations of Program Evaluation: Theories of Practice.* Thousand Oaks, Calif.: Sage, 1991.

Stake, R. E. *Standards-Based and Responsive Evaluation.* Thousand Oaks, Calif.: Sage, 2003.

Stufflebeam, D. L. "The CIPP Model for Evaluation." In T. Kellaghan and D. L. Stufflebeam (eds.), *The International Handbook of Educational Evaluation.* Norwood, Mass.: Kluwer, 2003.

Yin, R. *Case Study Research: Design and Methods.* Thousand Oaks, Calif.: Sage, 1989.

MARVIN C. ALKIN is an emeritus professor in the Social Research Methodology Division in the Graduate School of Education and Information Studies at University of California, Los Angeles.

CHRISTINA A. CHRISTIE is an assistant professor and associate director of the Institute of Organizational and Program Evaluation Research at Claremont Graduate University.

INDEX

Back Issue/Subscription Order Form

Copy or detach and send to:

Jossey-Bass, A Wiley Company, 989 Market Street, San Francisco CA 94103-1741

Call or fax toll-free: Phone 888-378-2537 6:30AM – 3PM PST; Fax 888-481-2665

Back Issues: Please send me the following issues at $29 each
(Important: please include series initials and issue number, such as EV101.)

_____

_____

_____

$ _____   Total for single issues

$ _____   SHIPPING CHARGES: SURFACE   Domestic   Canadian

	First Item	$5.00	$6.00
	Each Add'l Item	$3.00	$1.50

For next-day and second-day delivery rates, call the number listed above.

Subscriptions: Please __start __renew my subscription to *New Directions Evaluation*
for the year 2 _____ at the following rate:

U.S.	__Individual $80	__Institutional $175
Canada	__Individual $80	__Institutional $215
All Others	__Individual $104	__Institutional $249

**For more information about online subscriptions visit
www.interscience.wiley.com**

$ _____   Total single issues and subscriptions (Add appropriate sales tax
for your state for single issue orders. No sales tax for U.S.
subscriptions. Canadian residents, add GST for subscriptions and
single issues.)

__Payment enclosed (U.S. check or money order only)

__VISA __MC __AmEx #_____ Exp. Date _____

Signature _____ Day Phone _____

__ Bill Me (U.S. institutional orders only. Purchase order required.)

Purchase order # _____

Federal Tax ID13559302   **GST 89102 8052**

Name _____

Address _____

_____

Phone _____ E-mail _____

For more information about Jossey-Bass, visit our Web site at www.josseybass.com

OTHER TITLES AVAILABLE IN THE
NEW DIRECTIONS FOR EVALUATION SERIES
Jean A. King, Editor-in-Chief